LOCHLAINN SEABROOK WRITES ACROSS THE FOLLOWING GENRES & TOPICS

Academic	Earth Sciences	Illustrations	Poetry
Acoustic Culture	Ecology	Inspirational	Police Studies
Adventure	Ecotourism	Intellectual History	Politics
Aesthetics	Educational	Interdisciplinary Lost Knowledge	Practical Law
Alternate History	Encyclopediography	Interviews	Prehistoric Art
American Civil War	Entertainment	Journalism	Prehistoric Life
American History	Environmental History	Law Enforcement	Prehistory
American Politics	Environmental Science	Law of Attraction	Preservation Studies
American South	Environmental Studies	Legal Studies	Presidential History
American West	Environmental Tourism	Lexicography	Primatology
Anatomy and Physiology	Epistemology	Life After Death	Primary Documents
Ancient History	Ethnobotany	Life-Stage Biology	Prophecy
Animal Development	Ethnology	Lifestyle	Psychology
Antiquities	Ethology	Literary History	Public Safety
Anthologies	Ethnomusicology	Literature	Quiz
Anthropology	Ethnic Studies	Lost Intellectual Heritage	Quotations
Apocrypha	Etymology	Lost Knowledge Studies	Recollections
Aquariology	European History	Lost Treasures	Reference
Archaeology	Evolutionary Anthropology	Marine Biology	Religion
Art	Evolutionary Biology	Matriarchy	Revolutionary Period
Art History	Evolutionary History	Medical History	Science
Astronomy	Evolutionary Psychology	Memoir	Scripture
Aviation	Exploration	Men's Studies	Self-help
Aviation History	Exobiology	Metahistory	Social Sciences
Behavioral Science	Exposés	Metaphysics	Sociology
Biblical Exegesis	Family Histories	Military	Sound Studies
Biblical Hermeneutics	Field Guides	Military History	Southern Culture
Bioarchaeology	Film	Museum Studies	Southern Heritage
Biography	Folklore	Music History	Southern Narratives
Book History	Forestry	Musicology	Southern Studies
Botany	Genealogy	Mysteries and Enigmas	Southern Traditions
Camping	General Audience	Mysticism	Speeches
Children's Books	Geography	Mythology	Spirituality
Children's Natural History	Geology	National Parks	Spiritualism
Christian Mysticism	Genetics	Natural Health	Sport Science
Citizen's Rights Education	Ghost Stories	Natural History	Symbolism
Civil Liberties	Gospels	Natural Philosophy	Technology
Civil Rights Law	Guidebooks	Natural Science	Thanatology
Civil Self Defense	Handbooks	Nature	Theology
Clinical Studies	Health and Fitness	Nature Appreciation	Theosophy
Coffee Table Books	Heritage Conservation	Nature Art	Tourism
Coloring Books	Heritage Travel	Nonfiction	Travel
Comparative Aesthetics	Hiking	Oceanography	UFOlogy
Comparative Animal Development	Historical Ecology	Onomastics	United States
Comparative History	Historical Fiction	Ontogeny	Vanished Works Studies
Comparative Mythology	Historical Musicology	Outdoor Recreation	Vexillology
Comparative Religion	Historical Nonfiction	Paleoanthropology	Victorian Era Studies
Conservation	Historiography	Paleoecology	Victorian Medicine
Constitutional Law	History	Palography	Visual Arts
Constitutional Studies	History of Ideas	Paleoichthyology	Visual Cultural Memory Studies
Cooking	History of Medicine	Paleontology	Visual Encyclopediography
Criminal Justice	History of Science	Paleozoology	Visual Natural History
Criminal Procedure	History of Technology	Paranormal	War
Cryptozoology	Hobbies and Crafts	Parapsychology	Western Art Music History
Cultural Anthropology	Human-Animal Relationships	Parks & Campgrounds	Western Civilization
Cultural Geography	Human-Animal Studies	Patriarchy	Wildlife
Cultural Heritage	Human Evolution	Patriotism	Wildlife Biology
Cultural Heritage Studies	Humanities	Performing Arts	Wildlife Photography
Cultural History	Humor	Philosophical Aesthetics	Women's Studies
Cultural Studies	Ichthyology	Philosophy	World History
Cultural Tourism	Illustrated Lost History	Philosophy of Science	Writing
Deep Time Natural History	Illustrated Music History	Photography	Young Adult
Destination Guides	Illustrated Natural History	Physical Anthropology	Zoology
Diet and Nutrition	Illustrated Zoological Anthologies	Pictorial	

Mr. Seabrook does not author books for fame and glory, but for the love of writing and sharing his knowledge.

Be curious, not judgmental.

The 50 Greatest

NATIONAL PARKS

In The United States

*An Illustrated Guide to America's
Most Iconic Natural Treasures*

LOCHLAINN SEABROOK
Bestselling Author, Award-winning Historian, Acclaimed Artist

**Diligently Researched and Generously Illustrated
by the Author for the Elucidation of the Reader**

2025

Sea Raven Press, Park County, Wyoming USA

Published by
Sea Raven Press, LLC, founded 1995
Park County, Wyoming, USA
SeaRavenPress.com

All text, artwork, and illustrations copyright © Lochlainn Seabrook 2025
in accordance with U.S. and international copyright laws and regulations, as stated and protected under the Berne Union for the Protection of Literary and Artistic Property (Berne Convention), and the Universal Copyright Convention (the UCC). All rights reserved under the Pan-American and International Copyright Conventions.

PRINTING HISTORY
1st SRP paperback edition, 1st printing, November 2025 • ISBN: 978-1-955351-76-8
1st SRP hardcover edition, 1st printing, November 2025 • ISBN: 978-1-955351-77-5

ISBN: 978-1-955351-76-8 (paperback)
Library of Congress Control Number: 2026930910

This work is the copyrighted intellectual property of Lochlainn Seabrook and has been registered with the Copyright Office at the Library of Congress in Washington, D.C., USA. No part of this work (including text, covers, drawings, photos, illustrations, maps, images, diagrams, etc.), in whole or in part, may be used, reproduced, stored in a retrieval system, or transmitted, in any form or by any means now known or hereafter invented, without written permission from the publisher. The sale, duplication, hire, lending, copying, digitalization, or reproduction of this material, in any manner or form whatsoever, is also prohibited, and is a violation of federal, civil, and digital copyright law, which provides severe civil and criminal penalties for any violations.

The 50 Greatest National Parks in the United States: An Illustrated Guide to America's Most Iconic Natural Treasures, by Lochlainn Seabrook. Includes an introduction, educational section, notes to the reader, and illustrations.

ARTWORK
Front and back cover design and art, book design, layout, font selection, and interior art by Lochlainn Seabrook.
All images, pictures, photos, illustrations, image captions, graphic design, and graphic art copyright © Lochlainn Seabrook.
All images created and/or selected, placed, manipulated, cleaned, colored, and tinted by Lochlainn Seabrook.
Cover image: "Grand Canyon of the Yellowstone," copyright © Lochlainn Seabrook.
All rights reserved.

All persons who approve of the authority and principles of Colonel Lochlainn Seabrook's literary work, and realize its benefits as a means of reeducating the world about facts left out of mainstream books, are hereby requested to avidly recommend his titles to others and to vigorously cooperate in extending their reach, scope, and influence around the globe.

The views documented in this book concerning America's 63 National Parks are those of the publisher.
PROUDLY WRITTEN, DESIGNED, AND PUBLISHED IN THE UNITED STATES OF AMERICA.

Dedication

To one of my favorite national parks, Yellowstone.

Old Faithful, Yellowstone National Park, Wyoming. Copyright © Lochlainn Seabrook.

Epigraph

"The tendency nowadays to wander in wildernesses is delightful to see. Thousands of tired, nerve-shaken, over-civilized people are beginning to find out that going to the mountains is going home; that wildness is a necessity; and that mountain parks and reservations are useful not only as fountains of timber and irrigating rivers, but as fountains of life."

John Muir
Our National Parks, 1901

John Muir in his prime, circa 1880. Copyright © Lochlainn Seabrook.

CONTENTS

Notes to the Reader 〰 page 11
The Benefits of Visiting National Parks, by Lochlainn Seabrook 〰 page 12
Introduction, by Lochlainn Seabrook 〰 page 13

1. Acadia National Park: Maine 〰 page 16
2. Arches National Park: Utah 〰 page 18
3. Badlands National Park: South Dakota 〰 page 20
4. Big Bend National Park: Texas 〰 page 22
5. Biscayne National Park: Florida 〰 page 24
6. Bryce Canyon National Park: Utah 〰 page 26
7. Canyonlands National Park: Utah 〰 page 28
8. Capitol Reef National Park: Utah 〰 page 30
9. Carlsbad Caverns National Park: New Mexico 〰 page 32
10. Channel Islands National Park: California 〰 page 34
11. Congaree National Park: South Carolina 〰 page 36
12. Crater Lake National Park: Oregon 〰 page 38
13. Cuyahoga Valley National Park: Ohio 〰 page 40
14. Death Valley National Park: California & Nevada 〰 page 42
15. Denali National Park & Preserve: Alaska 〰 page 44
16. Dry Tortugas National Park: Florida 〰 page 46
17. Everglades National Park: Florida 〰 page 48
18. Glacier Bay National Park & Preserve: Alaska 〰 page 50
19. Glacier National Park: Montana 〰 page 52
20. Grand Canyon National Park: Arizona 〰 page 54
21. Grand Teton National Park: Wyoming 〰 page 56
22. Great Sand Dunes National Park & Preserve: Colorado 〰 page 58
23. Great Smoky Mountains National Park: Tennessee & North Carolina 〰 page 60
24. Guadalupe Mountains National Park: Texas 〰 page 62
25. Haleakalā National Park: Hawaii 〰 page 64
26. Hawai'i Volcanoes National Park: Hawaii 〰 page 66
27. Hot Springs National Park: Arkansas 〰 page 68
28. Indiana Dunes National Park: Indiana 〰 page 70
29. Isle Royale National Park: Michigan 〰 page 72
30. Joshua Tree National Park: California 〰 page 74
31. Kenai Fjords National Park: Alaska 〰 page 76
32. Lassen Volcanic National Park: California 〰 page 78
33. Mammoth Cave National Park: Kentucky 〰 page 80
34. Mesa Verde National Park: Colorado 〰 page 82

35. Mount Rainier National Park: Washington ❧ page 84
36. North Cascades National Park: Washington ❧ page 86
37. Olympic National Park: Washington ❧ page 88
38. Petrified Forest National Park: Arizona ❧ page 90
39. Redwood National & State Parks: California ❧ page 92
40. Rocky Mountain National Park: Colorado ❧ page 94
41. Saguaro National Park: Arizona ❧ page 96
42. Sequoia National Park: California ❧ page 98
43. Shenandoah National Park: Virginia ❧ page 100
44. Theodore Roosevelt National Park: North Dakota ❧ page 102
45. Voyageurs National Park: Minnesota ❧ page 104
46. White Sands National Park: New Mexico ❧ page 106
47. Wind Cave National Park: South Dakota ❧ page 108
48. Yellowstone National Park: Wyoming, Montana, & Idaho ❧ page 110
49. Yosemite National Park: California ❧ page 112
50. Zion National Park: Utah ❧ page 114

Honorable Mentions ❧ page 116
Meet the Author-Historian-Artist ❧ page 117
Praise for the Author ❧ page 119
Learn More ❧ page 123

Thor's Hammer, Bryce Canyon National Park, Utah. Copyright © Lochlainn Seabrook.

Notes to the Reader

MY SOURCES
☛ Consistent with all of my nature-oriented works, this book draws exclusively on the most current and reliable data available. Every effort has been made to ensure accuracy, objectivity, and freedom from speculation or bias.

MY RESEARCH
☛ Because of the inherent challenges in geography, geology, climatology, and ecology, complete scientific consensus is not always possible. For this reason, some data presented here may differ from that found in other nature or park-related sources. In certain cases specific figures have been carefully estimated where definitive values remain uncertain.

PARK COORDINATES
☛ The latitude and longitude listed for each national park in this volume represent the official geographic centroids recognized by the National Park Service. Because each park encompasses vast and irregular terrain, these coordinates are not intended to mark boundaries, but rather to indicate the park's approximate central point for reference. In other words, they offer readers a consistent and accurate means of locating the park's general position on a map.

DISCLAIMER
☛ The information in this book has been compiled from reputable sources, including the National Park Service, the U.S. Geological Survey, and the National Oceanic and Atmospheric Administration. While I have attempted to ensure accuracy and currency, natural conditions, regulations, and park accessibility may change without notice. The author and publisher assume no responsibility for any loss, injury, or inconvenience sustained by anyone using this book or relying on its contents. Readers are advised to verify all information with official park authorities before visiting. By using this book, readers acknowledge that they do so at their own risk and assume full responsibility for their actions and decisions.

L. Seabrook

LEAVE NO TRACE
☛ Visitors are encouraged to follow the Leave No Trace principles of outdoor ethics: respect wildlife, stay on designated trails, carry out all litter, and leave natural and cultural features undisturbed. Every small act of care helps preserve America's national parks for future generations.

WILDLIFE SAFETY
☛ All wild animals, regardless of size or apparent tameness, are unpredictable and potentially dangerous. Maintain safe distances at all times, never feed wildlife, and observe quietly to ensure both visitor safety and animal well-being.

CONSERVATION
☛ Each national park exists to protect irreplaceable landscapes, ecosystems, and species. Visitors share in this stewardship by minimizing impact, supporting responsible park management, and fostering an appreciation for the natural world through knowledge and respect.

The Benefits of Visiting National Parks

Visiting America's national parks offers far more than scenic beauty. Time spent in wild places restores physical health, reduces stress, sharpens the senses, and renews mental clarity. Immersion in natural light and fresh air supports the body's rhythms, while walking and hiking strengthen both heart and mind.

Yet the value of the parks extends beyond personal well-being. They safeguard the finest expressions of America's natural and cultural heritage—living classrooms and sanctuaries of wildness where our children and grandchildren can experience the unspoiled landscapes that shaped our history and identity.

Each visit fosters environmental awareness, deepens respect for the land and its wildlife, and renews our understanding of why preservation matters. To explore these protected places is to participate in their stewardship, ensuring that the natural world, and the spirit it awakens in us, continues for centuries to come.

The parks also remind us that wilderness is not a luxury but a necessity. In a fast-paced, technology-driven world, the quiet rhythm of wind, water, and wildlife reconnects us to the natural order from which all civilization springs. Standing before a mountain range or beneath a canopy of stars restores a sense of humility and wonder that no artificial environment can provide.

Our national parks belong to everyone. They are a shared inheritance—preserved through foresight, courage, and sacrifice—offering each visitor an opportunity to experience the best of America's landscapes and spirit. In protecting them we honor those who came before us, while fulfilling our duty to those yet to come, ensuring that these irreplaceable wonders remain a living legacy for future generations. L.S.

Teton Range viewed from Bridger-Teton National Forest, Wyoming. Copyright © Lochlainn Seabrook.

INTRODUCTION

As a nature writer, outdoorsman, photographer, and filmmaker, my connection to the American landscape runs deep. I have spent much of my life in and around the mountains, forests, deserts, and coasts that shape our country's wild character. The national parks stand as its finest expression—unspoiled, untamed, and honest. They are not museums or monuments. They are living pieces of America itself.

I wrote this book not to repeat what has already been said, but to look at the parks as they truly are. Each one has its own identity, its own terrain, its own weather, its own story. Together they form a map of the United States; not the one you see in an atlas, but one drawn by millennia in rock, water, and wind.

Bull elk leading its herd, Rocky Mountain National Park, Colorado. Copyright © Lochlainn Seabrook.

Through the years I have explored many of these places, often alone with camera and notebook. Standing in a canyon at sunrise or on a ridge after a storm, one gains a unique perspective that goes beyond photographs, travel guides, and tourist traps. Our national parks have a way of cutting through both the noise and the human ego. They reveal the presence of something far greater than ourselves, something ineffable, even transcendent.

The 50 Greatest National Parks in the United States is not a tourist guide or a sightseeing catalog. It is a field companion and a record, drawn from verified data, direct experience, and an abiding respect for wildness itself. My goal is simple: to present these places clearly and accurately, and to honor them for what they represent—the last natural wonders of a vast and rapidly changing world.

Lochlainn Seabrook
Park County, Wyoming, USA
November 2025

"Books invite all; they constrain none."
Hartley Burr Alexander (1873-1939)

The 50 Greatest
NATIONAL PARKS
in the United States

"Leave it as it is. You cannot improve on it. The ages have been at work on it, and man can only mar it. What you can do is to keep it for your children, your children's children, and for all who come after you, as one of the great sights which every American if he can travel at all should see."

Theodore Roosevelt, 1903

(on a visit to the Grand Canyon prior to it being designated a national park)

ACADIA NATIONAL PARK

OFFICIAL NAME: Acadia National Park.
STATE: Maine.
DESIGNATION: National Park; est. 1919.
COORDINATES: 44.35° N, 68.21° W.
TOTAL AREA: ~49,000 acres.
ELEVATION RANGE: Sea level–1,530 ft. at Cadillac Mountain.
ANNUAL VISITORS: ~3.9 million.
OPERATING SEASON: Yr-round; busiest May–Oct.
GOVERNING BODY: National Park Service.
MAIN ENTRANCES / GATEWAYS: Bar Harbor, Hulls Cove VC, and Park Loop Rd.
PRIMARY LANDSCAPE TYPE: Rocky coast, granite peaks, glacial lakes, and conifer forest.
MAJOR NATURAL LANDMARKS: Cadillac Mountain, Jordan Pond, Thunder Hole, Otter Cliffs, and Sand Beach.
SIGNATURE WILDLIFE: White-tailed deer, red fox, peregrine falcon, bald eagle, and harbor seal.
VEGETATION ZONES: N. hardwood and boreal forest with alpine and coastal flora.
CLIMATE: Humid continental; cool 70s °F summers, cold snowy winters; frequent fog.
UNIQUE GEOLOGY / ECOSYSTEM: Glaciers shaped granite mtns and valleys, forming compact marine, wetland, and alpine habitats rich in biodiversity.
INDIGENOUS HERITAGE: Homeland of the Wabanaki; they called the island Pemetic, "sloping land." Their traditions remain tied to the region's rivers and coasts.
HISTORIC SIGNIFICANCE: Protected in 1919 as Lafayette National Park; renamed Acadia in 1929; first park east of the Mississippi.
FAMOUS LANDMARKS / TRAILS: Cadillac Summit Rd, Beehive and Precipice Trails, Jordan Pond Path, and 45 mi. Carriage Rd. system.
WHAT IT'S KNOWN FOR: Rugged Atlantic coast, granite mountains, dramatic sunrises, and high ecological diversity.
ACTIVITIES: Hiking, driving, cycling, kayaking, wildlife viewing, and winter skiing.
AVERAGE VISIT DURATION: ~2 days.
VISITOR TIPS: Summer traffic heavy; arrive early; use Island Explorer shuttle; pack layers for fast weather shifts.
HIGHLIGHT: Sunrise from Cadillac Mountain, among the first U.S. points to greet daylight.

Otter Point, Acadia National Park, Maine. Copyright © Lochlainn Seabrook.

ARCHES NATIONAL PARK

OFFICIAL NAME: Arches National Park.
STATE: Utah.
DESIGNATION: Designated a National Monument in 1929 and a National Park in 1971.
COORDINATES: Approx. 38°40 N, 109°34 W.
TOTAL AREA: 76,519 acres (119 sq mi).
ELEVATION RANGE: 4,085–5,653 ft.
ANNUAL VISITORS: About 1.48 million (2023).
OPERATING SEASON: Open year-round; busiest March through October.
GOVERNING BODY: U.S. Department of the Interior – National Park Service.
MAIN ENTRANCES / GATEWAYS: Main entrance off U.S. 191 five miles north of Moab.
PRIMARY LANDSCAPE TYPE: High-desert sandstone terrain of arches, fins, and buttes.
MAJOR NATURAL LANDMARKS: Over 2,000 arches including Delicate Arch and Landscape Arch.
SIGNATURE WILDLIFE: Desert bighorn sheep, mule deer, collared lizards, and raptors.
VEGETATION ZONES: Pinyon-juniper woodland, sagebrush, and cryptobiotic soil crusts.
CLIMATE: Arid with hot summers, cold winters, and under 10 inches of annual rainfall.
UNIQUE GEOLOGY / ECOSYSTEM: Formed by collapse of the Salt Valley anticline and erosion of Entrada and Navajo Sandstone.
INDIGENOUS HERITAGE: Long used by Ute and Paiute peoples whose petroglyphs remain throughout the region.
HISTORIC SIGNIFICANCE: Protected in 1929 for its geology and reclassified in 1971 to preserve its remarkable formations.
FAMOUS LANDMARKS / TRAILS: Delicate Arch, Devil's Garden, The Windows, Double Arch, and Balanced Rock.
WHAT IT'S KNOWN FOR: The world's densest concentration of natural stone arches and iconic desert scenery.
ACTIVITIES: Hiking, sightseeing, photography, stargazing, and camping.
AVERAGE VISIT DURATION: 1–2 days depending on interest and season.
VISITOR TIPS: Arrive early, carry water, and avoid off-trail walking on fragile desert soil.
HIGHLIGHT: Delicate Arch glowing crimson at sunset remains one of the most enduring symbols of the American Southwest.

Delicate Arch, Arches National Park, Utah. Copyright © Lochlainn Seabrook.

BADLANDS NATIONAL PARK

OFFICIAL NAME: Badlands National Park.
STATE: South Dakota.
DESIGNATION: National Park; est. 1978.
COORDINATES: 43.855° N, 102.339° W.
TOTAL AREA: 242,756 acres.
ELEVATION RANGE: 2,460–3,282 ft.
ANNUAL VISITORS: About 1 million.
OPERATING SEASON: Year-round; busiest May–September.
GOVERNING BODY: National Park Service.
MAIN ENTRANCES / GATEWAYS: Wall, Interior, and Scenic, South Dakota, via Highway 240 and I-90.
PRIMARY LANDSCAPE TYPE: Eroded badlands and mixed-grass prairie.
MAJOR NATURAL LANDMARKS: The Pinnacles, Yellow Mounds, Big Badlands Overlook, Sage Creek Wilderness.
SIGNATURE WILDLIFE: Bison, bighorn sheep, pronghorn, prairie dogs, and coyotes.
VEGETATION ZONES: Prairie grasses with sagebrush, juniper, and cottonwood.
CLIMATE: Semi-arid; hot summers near 90 °F, cold winters below 20 °F; about 16 in. of annual precipitation.
UNIQUE GEOLOGY / ECOSYSTEM: Strata of clay, silt, and ash expose fossils 75–28 million years old. Erosion forms spires and ridges revealing ancient species once native to the region.
INDIGENOUS HERITAGE: The Lakota Sioux, calling it *mako sica* ("bad land"), regard it as sacred ground for hunting and vision quests.
HISTORIC SIGNIFICANCE: Inhabited for over 11,000 years, later ranched and used as a World War II gunnery range. Fossils and artifacts trace life across eons.
FAMOUS LANDMARKS / TRAILS: Notch Trail, Door Trail, Castle Trail, and Sage Creek Rim Road.
WHAT IT'S KNOWN FOR: Color-banded cliffs, fossils, open prairies, and vivid sunsets.
ACTIVITIES: Driving, hiking, camping, wildlife viewing, and stargazing.
AVERAGE VISIT DURATION: ½ day–1 day.
VISITOR TIPS: Bring water and sunscreen. Expect wind and fast-changing weather.
HIGHLIGHT: A stark fossil-laden wilderness of sculpted stone and prairie grass, Badlands National Park reveals the living history of deep geologic time.

Sunrise at Badlands National Park, South Dakota. Copyright © Lochlainn Seabrook.

BIG BEND NATIONAL PARK

OFFICIAL NAME: Big Bend National Park.
STATE: Texas.
DESIGNATION: National Park; est. 1944.
COORDINATES: 29.25° N, 103.25° W.
TOTAL AREA: 801,163 acres.
ELEVATION RANGE: 1,715–7,832 ft.
ANNUAL VISITORS: Around 520,000.
OPERATING SEASON: Open year-round; spring and fall most popular.
GOVERNING BODY: National Park Service.
MAIN ENTRANCES / GATEWAYS: Panther Junction, Rio Grande Village, and Maverick Junction near Terlingua.
PRIMARY LANDSCAPE TYPE: Chihuahuan Desert basin framed by the Chisos Mountains and the Rio Grande.
MAJOR NATURAL LANDMARKS: Santa Elena Canyon, Boquillas Canyon, Emory Peak, and the Window.
SIGNATURE WILDLIFE: Black bear, mountain lion, javelina, roadrunner, and golden eagle.
VEGETATION ZONES: Desert scrub, grassland, riparian woodland, and mountain forest.
CLIMATE: Arid to semi-arid; desert highs above 100 °F in summer, cool mountain nights year-round.
UNIQUE GEOLOGY / ECOSYSTEM: Displays 500 million years of geologic history; ancient marine sediments, volcanic formations, and desert flora sustain exceptional biodiversity.
INDIGENOUS HERITAGE: Once inhabited by Chisos, Jumano, and Mescalero Apache peoples; petroglyphs and campsites attest to their presence.
HISTORIC SIGNIFICANCE: Served as a trade and travel corridor for Native and Mexican peoples; later ranching and mining lands before preservation in 1944.
FAMOUS LANDMARKS / TRAILS: Lost Mine Trail, South Rim Trail, Santa Elena Canyon Trail, and Ross Maxwell Scenic Drive.
WHAT IT'S KNOWN FOR: Vast desert vistas, rugged canyons, and some of the darkest night skies in the continental U.S.
ACTIVITIES: Hiking, birding, rafting, scenic driving, camping, and photography.
VISITOR TIPS: Carry fuel and water; cell service is limited; avoid summer midday heat; best months November–April.
HIGHLIGHT: The Chisos Mountains rise dramatically from the desert floor, offering panoramic views across the Rio Grande into Mexico's Sierra del Carmen.

The Rio Grande, Big Bend National Park, Texas. Copyright © Lochlainn Seabrook.

BISCAYNE NATIONAL PARK

OFFICIAL NAME: Biscayne National Park.
STATE: Florida.
DESIGNATION: National Park; est. 1980.
COORDINATES: 25.48°N, 80.21°W.
TOTAL AREA: 172,971 acres.
ELEVATION RANGE: Sea level–10 ft.
ANNUAL VISITORS: About 700,000.
OPERATING SEASON: Year-round.
GOVERNING BODY: National Park Service.
MAIN ENTRANCES / GATEWAYS: Dante Fascell Visitor Center, Homestead.
PRIMARY LANDSCAPE TYPE: Subtropical marine and coastal ecosystem.
MAJOR NATURAL LANDMARKS: Elliott Key, Boca Chita Key, and Biscayne Bay.
SIGNATURE WILDLIFE: Manatees, dolphins, pelicans, sea turtles, and tropical fish.
VEGETATION ZONES: Mangroves, seagrass meadows, and coral reef habitats.
CLIMATE: Tropical; hot wet summers, warm dry winters; hurricanes possible June–Nov.
UNIQUE GEOLOGY / ECOSYSTEM: Built on coral limestone and mangrove peat; BNP is the only U.S. park that protects mangroves, seagrass, and living coral reef together.
INDIGENOUS HERITAGE: Home of the Tequesta for thousands of years; artifacts and shell middens found on nearby keys reveal a thriving coastal culture.
HISTORIC SIGNIFICANCE: Spanish explorers sailed here in the 1500s; reefs caused many shipwrecks; homesteaders later farmed tropical fruit before the area was preserved.
FAMOUS LANDMARKS / TRAILS: Boca Chita Lighthouse, Jones Lagoon Kayak Route, the Maritime Heritage Trail of shipwrecks.
WHAT IT'S KNOWN FOR: Clear turquoise waters, coral reefs, mangrove forests, and abundant marine life beneath the surface.
ACTIVITIES: Boating, snorkeling, scuba diving, kayaking, paddleboarding, and birdwatching.
AVERAGE VISIT DURATION: 1 day.
VISITOR TIPS: Reach by private boat or guided tour; mornings offer best visibility; carry water, sunscreen, and insect repellent.
HIGHLIGHT: The park protects the tropical heart of southern Florida, where mangroves, shallow bay, and coral reef meet in one seamless, living marine wilderness.

Biscayne National Park, Florida. Copyright © Lochlainn Seabrook.

BRYCE CANYON NATIONAL PARK

OFFICIAL NAME: Bryce Canyon National Park.
STATE: Utah.
DESIGNATION: National Park; est. 1928.
COORDINATES: 37.5930° N, 112.1871° W.
TOTAL AREA: 35,835 acres.
ELEVATION RANGE: 6,620–9,115 ft.
ANNUAL VISITORS: About 2.3 million per year.
OPERATING SEASON: Open year-round; snow may limit winter access.
GOVERNING BODY: National Park Service.
MAIN ENTRANCES / GATEWAYS: Utah State Route 63 near Bryce Canyon City.
PRIMARY LANDSCAPE TYPE: Plateau amphitheaters of eroded sedimentary rock and vivid hoodoos.
MAJOR NATURAL LANDMARKS: Bryce Amphitheater, Rainbow Point, Inspiration Point, Sunset Point.
SIGNATURE WILDLIFE: Mule deer, pronghorns, peregrine falcons, mountain lions, and ravens.
VEGETATION ZONES: Pinyon-juniper woodland, ponderosa pine, and aspen-fir forest.
CLIMATE: High-plateau continental climate with warm days, cold nights, and snowy winters.
UNIQUE GEOLOGY / ECOSYSTEM: A chain of natural amphitheaters carved from the Claron Formation, famed for dense clusters of hoodoos formed by frost-wedging and rain erosion.
INDIGENOUS HERITAGE: Long inhabited by the Northern Paiute, who saw the hoodoos as beings turned to stone.
HISTORIC SIGNIFICANCE: Designated a national monument in 1923 and upgraded to park status in 1928 to protect its singular landscape.
FAMOUS LANDMARKS / TRAILS: Queens Garden, Navajo Loop, Fairyland Loop, Rim Trail, and Rainbow Point Scenic Drive.
WHAT IT'S KNOWN FOR: Extraordinary hoodoos, red-orange cliffs, and dramatic light at sunrise and sunset.
ACTIVITIES: Hiking, scenic drives, horseback rides, photography, and world-class stargazing.
AVERAGE VISIT DURATION: ½ day–1 full day, depending on trail activity and sightseeing pace.
VISITOR TIPS: Dress in layers, start early, bring water, and use shuttles in peak season.
HIGHLIGHT: Dawn light striking the crimson hoodoos of Bryce Amphitheater beneath the clear Utah sky.

Bryce Amphitheater, Bryce Canyon National Park, Utah. Copyright © Lochlainn Seabrook.

CANYONLANDS NATIONAL PARK

OFFICIAL NAME: Canyonlands National Park.
STATE: Utah.
DESIGNATION: National Park; est. 1964.
COORDINATES: 38.20° N, 109.93° W.
TOTAL AREA: 337,598 acres.
ELEVATION RANGE: 3,700–7,200 ft.
ANNUAL VISITORS: About 800,000.
OPERATING SEASON: Year-round; busiest March–October.
GOVERNING BODY: National Park Service.
MAIN ENTRANCES / GATEWAYS: Island in the Sky (Moab), Needles District (Monticello), Maze District (Utah Hwy 24).
PRIMARY LANDSCAPE TYPE: High-desert plateau carved by the Colorado and Green Rivers.
MAJOR NATURAL LANDMARKS: Mesa Arch, Grand View Point, Upheaval Dome, White Rim, Needles spires.
SIGNATURE WILDLIFE: Desert bighorn sheep, mule deer, coyote, golden eagle, peregrine falcon, collared lizard.
VEGETATION ZONES: Pinyon–juniper woodland, blackbrush scrub, desert grassland, riparian cottonwoods.
CLIMATE: Arid continental; hot summers (90–105 °F), cold winters (20–40 °F), ~9 in. annual rainfall.
UNIQUE GEOLOGY / ECOSYSTEM: Multicolored sedimentary layers show 300 million years of uplift and erosion; deep canyons and arches carved by the Colorado Plateau's rivers.
INDIGENOUS HERITAGE: Once home to Ancestral Puebloans; rock art and granaries remain in Horseshoe Canyon; later used by Ute and Navajo peoples.
HISTORIC SIGNIFICANCE: Explored by trappers and ranchers in the 1800s; later mining and preservation led to park status in 1964.
FAMOUS LANDMARKS / TRAILS: Mesa Arch, White Rim Road, Druid Arch Trail, Chesler Park Loop, Maze Overlook.
WHAT IT'S KNOWN FOR: Vast red-rock panoramas, labyrinthine canyons, and the junction of the Colorado and Green Rivers.
ACTIVITIES: Hiking, mountain biking, canyoneering, rafting, and stargazing.
AVERAGE VISIT DURATION: 1–3 days.
VISITOR TIPS: Bring water and maps; few services; 4WD needed for Maze and White Rim; best light at sunrise and sunset.
HIGHLIGHT: From Island in the Sky's Grand View Point the desert wilderness stretches unbroken for hundreds of miles under endless sky.

Mesa Arch, Canyonlands National Park, Utah. Copyright © Lochlainn Seabrook.

CAPITOL REEF NATIONAL PARK

OFFICIAL NAME: Capitol Reef National Park.
STATE: Utah.
DESIGNATION: National Park; est. 1971.
COORDINATES: 38.20° N, 111.17° W.
TOTAL AREA: 241,904 acres.
ELEVATION RANGE: 3,880–8,960 ft.
ANNUAL VISITORS: About 1.3 million.
OPERATING SEASON: Open year-round; busiest spring to fall.
GOVERNING BODY: National Park Service.
MAIN ENTRANCES / GATEWAYS: Fruita on Utah Hwy 24; Notom-Bullfrog and Burr Trail roads.
PRIMARY LANDSCAPE TYPE: Arid canyonlands and uplifted monocline of the Colorado Plateau.
MAJOR NATURAL LANDMARKS: Waterpocket Fold, Capitol Dome, Hickman Bridge, Cathedral Valley, Chimney Rock.
SIGNATURE WILDLIFE: Mule deer, desert bighorn, golden eagle, coyote, gray fox, and various lizards.
VEGETATION ZONES: Cottonwood and willow along streams; sagebrush, juniper, and pine at higher elevations.
CLIMATE: Semi-arid with hot summers, cold winters, and low humidity; about 7 in. annual rainfall.
UNIQUE GEOLOGY / ECOSYSTEM: The 100-mile-long Waterpocket Fold reveals nearly 200 million years of layered strata shaped by uplift and erosion.
INDIGENOUS HERITAGE: Fremont people lived here A.D. 600–1300, leaving petroglyphs and dwellings; later used by Ute and Paiute for hunting.
HISTORIC SIGNIFICANCE: Settlers founded Fruita in the late 1800s, creating orchards that still produce fruit today.
FAMOUS LANDMARKS / TRAILS: Capitol Gorge, Cassidy Arch, Grand Wash, Cohab Canyon, Rim Overlook, Cathedral Valley Loop.
WHAT IT'S KNOWN FOR: Red cliffs, creamy domes, deep canyons, Fremont rock art, and preserved orchards.
ACTIVITIES: Hiking, scenic driving, backpacking, canyoneering, stargazing, fruit picking, and photography.
AVERAGE VISIT DURATION: 1–2 days.
VISITOR TIPS: Carry water, avoid narrow canyons during storms, and start early for cooler temperatures.
HIGHLIGHT: Capitol Reef's vast Waterpocket Fold displays a brilliant cross-section of the Colorado Plateau's ancient desert geology.

Capitol Dome overlooking the Fremont River, Capitol Reef National Park, Utah. Copyright © Lochlainn Seabrook.

CARLSBAD CAVERNS NATIONAL PARK

OFFICIAL NAME: Carlsbad Caverns National Park.
STATE: New Mexico.
DESIGNATION: National Park; est. 1930.
COORDINATES: 32.1479° N, 104.5567° W.
TOTAL AREA: 46,766 acres.
ELEVATION RANGE: 3,596–6,368 ft.
ANNUAL VISITORS: ~440,000.
OPERATING SEASON: Year-round; peak visitation in spring and fall.
GOVERNING BODY: National Park Service.
MAIN ENTRANCES / GATEWAYS: Carlsbad, Whites City, and U.S. Hwy 62/180.
PRIMARY LANDSCAPE TYPE: Arid limestone plateau within the northern Chihuahuan Desert.
MAJOR NATURAL LANDMARKS: Carlsbad Cavern, Lechuguilla Cave, and the Big Room.
SIGNATURE WILDLIFE: Brazilian free-tailed bats, mule deer, and ringtails.
VEGETATION ZONES: Desert scrub, sotol-grassland, and piñon-juniper woodland.
CLIMATE: Hot, dry summers; mild winters; annual rainfall about 14 in.
UNIQUE GEOLOGY / ECOSYSTEM: Carved from Permian limestone of the Capitan Reef by sulfuric acid, forming immense chambers with intricate speleothems and rare microbial colonies.
INDIGENOUS HERITAGE: Once known to the Mescalero Apache and earlier Jornada Mogollon peoples; ancient pictographs mark early human presence.
HISTORIC SIGNIFICANCE: First explored by Jim White in the 1890s. Declared a national monument in 1923 and park in 1930. Named a UNESCO World Heritage Site in 1995.
FAMOUS LANDMARKS / TRAILS: Big Room Trail, Natural Entrance Trail, and King's Palace.
WHAT IT'S KNOWN FOR: One of the world's largest and most ornate cave systems, famed for its giant subterranean chambers and bat flights.
ACTIVITIES: Cave tours, bat flight programs, hiking, and stargazing.
AVERAGE VISIT DURATION: 1–2 days.
VISITOR TIPS: Carry a light jacket; cave temperatures stay near 56 °F. Reserve guided tours in advance.
HIGHLIGHT: The dramatic nightly bat exodus from the Natural Entrance at dusk.

Stalactite and stalagmite formations inside the Big Room, Carlsbad Caverns National Park, New Mexico. Copyright © Lochlainn Seabrook.

CHANNEL ISLANDS NATIONAL PARK

OFFICIAL NAME: Channel Islands National Park.
STATE: California.
DESIGNATION: National Park; est. March 5, 1980.
COORDINATES: 34°0 N, 119°25 W.
TOTAL AREA: 249,561 acres.
ELEVATION RANGE: Sea level to approximately 2,450 ft. (Devils Peak on Santa Cruz Island).
OPERATING SEASON: Open year-round; island access depends on boat schedules and weather conditions.
GOVERNING BODY: National Park Service.
MAIN ENTRANCES / GATEWAYS: Ventura Harbor and Santa Barbara are primary mainland gateways; boat access by concession to the five islands.
PRIMARY LANDSCAPE TYPE: Remote marine archipelago of rugged coastal cliffs, sea caves, kelp forests, and open ocean waters.
MAJOR NATURAL LANDMARKS: Painted Cave on Santa Cruz Island, kelp-forest ecosystems, and uplifted marine terraces.
SIGNATURE WILDLIFE: Island fox, island scrub-jay, California sea lion, gray whale, and numerous seabirds and marine invertebrates.
VEGETATION ZONES: Grassland, coastal sage scrub, chaparral, oak woodland, riparian wetlands, and closed-cone conifer stands.
CLIMATE: Warm-summer Mediterranean with mild temperatures, frequent fog, and strong maritime winds.
UNIQUE GEOLOGY / ECOSYSTEM: Isolated islands with high endemism and marine terraces formed by uplift and sea-level change; a blend of terrestrial and marine ecosystems.
INDIGENOUS HERITAGE: The Chumash and Tongva peoples inhabited the islands for thousands of years, using plank canoes to trade and fish across the channel.
HISTORIC SIGNIFICANCE: Once used for ranching and maritime trade; now preserves a rare undeveloped Pacific coastal ecosystem and ancient archaeological sites.
WHAT IT'S KNOWN FOR: Known as the "Galápagos of North America" for its extraordinary biodiversity and isolation.
ACTIVITIES: Hiking, kayaking, snorkeling, diving, camping, wildlife viewing, photography, and boating.
VISITOR TIPS: Reserve boat tickets early, bring supplies and water, prepare for wind and rough seas, and Leave No Trace.
HIGHLIGHT: The wind-carved cliffs and vivid kelp-forest waters of Santa Cruz Island, California, where turquoise coves and sea arches showcase one of America's most pristine coastal wildernesses.

The sea cliffs of Santa Cruz Island, Channel Islands National Park, California. Copyright © Lochlainn Seabrook.

CONGAREE NATIONAL PARK

OFFICIAL NAME: Congaree National Park.
STATE: South Carolina.
DESIGNATION: Established as a national monument in 1976, redesignated a national park in 2003.
COORDINATES: 33.79° N, 80.77° W.
TOTAL AREA: 26,692 acres.
ELEVATION RANGE: 80–140 ft. above sea level.
ANNUAL VISITORS: Around 250,000 per year.
OPERATING SEASON: Open year-round; visitor center hours vary.
GOVERNING BODY: National Park Service.
PRIMARY LANDSCAPE TYPE: Floodplain hardwood forest shaped by the Congaree and Wateree Rivers.
MAJOR NATURAL LANDMARKS: Boardwalk Loop Trail, Cedar Creek Canoe Trail, and national champion trees over 150 ft. tall.
SIGNATURE WILDLIFE: White-tailed deer, river otter, wild turkey, barred owl, and prothonotary warbler.
VEGETATION ZONES: Bald cypress, tupelo, sweetgum, oak, and loblolly pine dominate flooded and upland areas.
CLIMATE: Humid subtropical with hot summers, mild winters, and periodic flooding from seasonal rains.
UNIQUE GEOLOGY / ECOSYSTEM: Flat alluvial plain with rich loam soils supporting one of the tallest temperate forest canopies in North America.
HISTORIC SIGNIFICANCE: Spared from logging and agriculture, the park preserves a rare old-growth tract once common across the Southeast.
FAMOUS LANDMARKS / TRAILS: Boardwalk Loop (2.4 mi.), Weston Lake Loop (4.4 mi.), and Cedar Creek Canoe Trail (≈15 mi.).
WHAT IT'S KNOWN FOR: Largest intact old-growth bottomland hardwood forest in the U.S., famed for towering trees, wildlife diversity, and quiet waterways.
ACTIVITIES: Hiking, canoeing, kayaking, birding, and wilderness camping in designated backcountry areas.
VISITOR TIPS: Expect mosquitoes and humidity; bring insect repellent; check flood conditions; spring and fall offer the best access.
HIGHLIGHT: A tranquil cathedral of immense hardwoods mirrored in still waters, Congaree preserves the last great floodplain forest of the American East—a living symbol of the South's original ancient wilderness.

Bald cypress trees (*Taxodium distichum*), Congaree National Park, South Carolina. Copyright © Lochlainn Seabrook.

CRATER LAKE NATIONAL PARK

OFFICIAL NAME: Crater Lake National Park.
STATE: Oregon.
DESIGNATION: National Park; est. 1902.
COORDINATES: 42.94° N, 122.10° W.
TOTAL AREA: 183,224 acres.
ELEVATION RANGE: 3,977–8,929 ft.
ANNUAL VISITORS: ~700,000.
OPERATING SEASON: Year-round, though heavy snow limits access Oct–May.
GOVERNING BODY: National Park Service.
MAIN ENTRANCES / GATEWAYS: South Entrance (via OR-62) and North Entrance (via OR-138).
PRIMARY LANDSCAPE TYPE: Volcanic caldera containing the deepest lake in the U.S.
MAJOR NATURAL LANDMARKS: Crater Lake, Wizard Island, Phantom Ship, and Rim Drive.
SIGNATURE WILDLIFE: Black bear, Roosevelt elk, mule deer, Clark's nutcracker, and bald eagle.
VEGETATION ZONES: Montane and subalpine forests with alpine meadows and pumice plains.
CLIMATE: Long snowy winters and short, mild summers with clear skies and crisp mornings.
UNIQUE GEOLOGY / ECOSYSTEM: Formed by the collapse of Mount Mazama about 7,700 years ago; the lake is 1,943 ft. deep and among the clearest on Earth.
INDIGENOUS HERITAGE: Sacred to the Klamath people, whose oral history recounts a great eruption born of divine conflict.
HISTORIC SIGNIFICANCE: Established to protect its purity and geologic grandeur; it became a model for later volcanic research and preservation.
FAMOUS LANDMARKS / TRAILS: Rim Drive, Cleetwood Cove Trail, Garfield Peak Trail, and Mount Scott Trail.
WHAT IT'S KNOWN FOR: Brilliant blue water ringed by cliffs and evergreen forest, visible from every rim viewpoint.
ACTIVITIES: Scenic drives, hiking, snowshoeing, and summer lake tours.
AVERAGE VISIT DURATION: 1–2 days.
VISITOR TIPS: Snow often lingers into July; check road conditions; bring layers, water, and sun protection.
HIGHLIGHT: Crater Lake's sapphire surface and surrounding caldera create one of the most breathtaking volcanic vistas in the United States.

Wizard Island, Crater Lake National Park, Oregon. Copyright © Lochlainn Seabrook.

CUYAHOGA VALLEY NATIONAL PARK

OFFICIAL NAME: Cuyahoga Valley National Park.
STATE: Ohio.
DESIGNATION: National Park; est. 2000.
COORDINATES: 41.24° N, 81.55° W.
TOTAL AREA: 32,572 acres.
ELEVATION RANGE: 590–1,210 ft.
ANNUAL VISITORS: About 2.9 million.
OPERATING SEASON: Year-round.
GOVERNING BODY: National Park Service.
MAIN ENTRANCES / GATEWAYS: Peninsula, Boston Mills, Brecksville.
PRIMARY LANDSCAPE TYPE: Glaciated river valley of forest, meadow, and wetland.
MAJOR NATURAL LANDMARKS: Brandywine Falls, Cuyahoga River, Beaver Marsh, Ledges Overlook.
SIGNATURE WILDLIFE: White-tailed deer, beaver, red fox, barred owl, great blue heron, bald eagle.
VEGETATION ZONES: Hardwood forest with oak, maple, and beech; wetlands with cattails and sedges; meadows with goldenrod and milkweed.
CLIMATE: Humid continental with cold winters, warm summers, and year-round precipitation.
UNIQUE GEOLOGY / ECOSYSTEM: Glacial retreat carved sandstone and shale bluffs, creating fertile floodplains that support diverse Great Lakes flora and fauna.
INDIGENOUS HERITAGE: Erie, Ottawa, and Wyandot peoples lived and traveled along the Cuyahoga River for millennia.
HISTORIC SIGNIFICANCE: The 1820s Ohio and Erie Canal made the valley a key trade route linking Lake Erie and the Ohio River; later restoration returned it to natural health.
FAMOUS LANDMARKS / TRAILS: Towpath Trail, Brandywine Gorge Trail, Ledges Trail.
WHAT IT'S KNOWN FOR: Scenic waterfalls, wooded valleys, and trails combining nature and history near Cleveland and Akron.
ACTIVITIES: Hiking, biking, birding, photography, kayaking, and train rides on the Cuyahoga Valley Scenic Railroad.
AVERAGE VISIT DURATION: 1–2 days.
VISITOR TIPS: Begin at Boston Mill Visitor Center; weekends are busy; fall color peaks in October; spring brings wildflowers along the riverbanks.
HIGHLIGHT: The 65-ft. Brandywine Falls, flowing through Berea Sandstone, captures the renewed spirit and natural beauty of Ohio's only national park.

Brandywine Falls, Cuyahoga Valley National Park, Ohio. Copyright © Lochlainn Seabrook.

DEATH VALLEY NATIONAL PARK

OFFICIAL NAME: Death Valley National Park.
STATES: California and Nevada.
DESIGNATION: National Park; est. 1994.
COORDINATES: 36.5323° N, 116.9325° W.
TOTAL AREA: 3,422,024 acres.
ELEVATION RANGE: −282 ft. at Badwater Basin to 11,043 ft. at Telescope Peak.
ANNUAL VISITORS: About 1.1 million.
OPERATING SEASON: Year-round; best October through April.
GOVERNING BODY: National Park Service.
MAIN ENTRANCES / GATEWAYS: Furnace Creek, Stovepipe Wells, Panamint Springs, Shoshone, Beatty.
PRIMARY LANDSCAPE TYPE: Arid desert basin bordered by rugged mountain ranges.
MAJOR NATURAL LANDMARKS: Badwater Basin, Zabriskie Point, Dante's View, Mesquite Flat Sand Dunes, Ubehebe Crater.
SIGNATURE WILDLIFE: Desert bighorn sheep, coyote, kit fox, chuckwalla, sidewinder rattlesnake, roadrunner, golden eagle.
VEGETATION ZONES: Creosote bush scrub, saltbush flats, mesquite groves, pinyon-juniper woodlands, bristlecone pine forests.
CLIMATE: Hottest and driest place in North America; summer highs above 120 °F, mild winters, annual rainfall 2 ins.
UNIQUE GEOLOGY / ECOSYSTEM: A vast basin of salt flats, dunes, craters, and fault-block mountains revealing over 500 million years of exposed geologic history.
INDIGENOUS HERITAGE: Inhabited by the Timbisha Shoshone, who survived through water knowledge, plant use, and seasonal migration; their village remains near Furnace Creek.
HISTORIC SIGNIFICANCE: Named by 1849 pioneers; later a borax mining hub symbolized by 20 Mule Team wagons; protected in 1933, elevated to park status in 1994.
WHAT IT'S KNOWN FOR: Record heat, immense salt flats, and dramatic desert scenery.
ACTIVITIES: Scenic drives, hiking, photography, geology study, and stargazing.
VISITOR TIPS: Carry water, fuel, and maps; avoid midday heat; check road conditions; explore early morning for best light and cooler temperatures.
HIGHLIGHT: From Badwater Basin, 282 ft. below sea level, visitors can see snowcapped Telescope Peak towering above—a striking contrast of desert extremes.

Badwater Basin salt flats, Death Valley National Park, California. Copyright © Lochlainn Seabrook.

DENALI NATIONAL PARK & PRESERVE

OFFICIAL NAME: Denali National Park and Preserve.
STATE: Alaska.
DESIGNATION: National Park and Preserve; est. 1917.
COORDINATES: 63.1148° N, 151.1926° W.
TOTAL AREA: 6,075,107 acres.
ELEVATION RANGE: 200–20,310 ft.
ANNUAL VISITORS: ~600,000.
OPERATING SEASON: Year-round; main access May–Sept.
GOVERNING BODY: National Park Service.
MAIN ENTRANCES / GATEWAYS: Denali Park Rd via George Parks Hwy from Anchorage or Fairbanks.
PRIMARY LANDSCAPE TYPE: Alpine tundra, boreal forest, glacial valleys, and rugged mountains.
MAJOR NATURAL LANDMARKS: Denali (Mt. McKinley), Muldrow Glacier, Wonder Lake, Toklat River.
SIGNATURE WILDLIFE: Grizzly bear, moose, Dall sheep, caribou, wolf, red fox, golden eagle.
VEGETATION ZONES: Taiga at lower elevations, tundra above tree line, alpine flora at peaks.
CLIMATE: Subarctic; long cold winters, short cool summers, dramatic temperature shifts.
UNIQUE GEOLOGY / ECOSYSTEM: Active tectonic uplift, braided glacial rivers, permafrost, and vast intact predator-prey ecosystems.
INDIGENOUS HERITAGE: Homeland of the Koyukon, Tanana, and Dena'ina Athabascans, whose traditions and place names remain integral to the region.
HISTORIC SIGNIFICANCE: Created to protect Dall sheep and mountain ecosystems; exploration and mountaineering history central to park identity.
FAMOUS LANDMARKS / TRAILS: Denali Summit, Savage River Loop, Eielson Visitor Center, McKinley Bar Trail.
WHAT IT'S KNOWN FOR: North America's highest peak, pristine wilderness, and minimal human infrastructure.
ACTIVITIES: Wildlife viewing, backcountry trekking, mountaineering, photography, and flightseeing.
AVERAGE VISIT DURATION: 2–3 days.
VISITOR TIPS: Private vehicles restricted beyond Mile 15; shuttle or bus access required; weather changes rapidly.
HIGHLIGHT: Denali's immense scale and raw solitude reveal the last great frontier of subarctic wilderness, where nature still reigns and silence overwhelms the landscape. Visitors experience a renewed sense of Earth's grandeur and timelessness.

Autumn on the Toklat River, Denali National Park, Alaska. Copyright © Lochlainn Seabrook.

DRY TORTUGAS NATIONAL PARK

OFFICIAL NAME: Dry Tortugas National Park.
STATE: Florida.
DESIGNATION: National Park; redesignated from Fort Jefferson National Monument in 1992.
COORDINATES: 24.63° N, 82.87° W.
TOTAL AREA: About 64,700 acres (roughly 100 sq. mi.).
ELEVATION RANGE: Sea level to abt. 10 ft. on Loggerhead Key.
ANNUAL VISITORS: Around 84,000 per year.
OPERATING SEASON: Year-round access by boat or seaplane from Key West.
GOVERNING BODY: National Park Service.
PRIMARY LANDSCAPE TYPE: Coral-sand islands ringed by reefs and seagrass meadows within open Gulf waters.
MAJOR NATURAL LANDMARKS: Fort Jefferson, Loggerhead Key, Garden Key, and Bush Key.
SIGNATURE WILDLIFE: Sea turtles, reef fish, sooty terns, brown noddies, and reef sharks.
VEGETATION ZONES: Salt-tolerant shrubs, mangroves, and underwater seagrasses.
CLIMATE: Tropical maritime; warm all year with wet summers and mild, breezy winters.
UNIQUE GEOLOGY / ECOSYSTEM: Coral reef and oolitic limestone formation marking the edge of the Florida Platform; reefs shelter abundant marine life and absorb storm energy.
INDIGENOUS HERITAGE: Visited by Native Caribbean peoples long before Europeans; named by Spaniards for its turtles and lack of fresh water.
HISTORIC SIGNIFICANCE: Home to 19th-Century Fort Jefferson, one of America's great coastal fortifications. It served as a military outpost and later a prison during and after the War Between the States; Southern leader Jefferson Davis was briefly confined here after the War Between the States before transfer to Virginia.
WHAT IT'S KNOWN FOR: Isolation, turquoise waters, coral reefs, bird colonies, and its massive brick fortress rising from the sea.
ACTIVITIES: Snorkeling, diving, bird-watching, photography, camping, and fort exploration.
VISITOR TIPS: Book transport early, bring all provisions, and follow park rules protecting nesting birds and coral reefs.
HIGHLIGHT: A tranquil Southern ocean sanctuary where tropical wilderness and 19th-Century history meet on the warm shores of the Gulf of America.

Fort Jefferson, Dry Tortugas National Park, Gulf of America, Florida. Copyright © Lochlainn Seabrook.

EVERGLADES NATIONAL PARK

OFFICIAL NAME: Everglades National Park.
STATE: Florida.
DESIGNATION: National Park; est. 1947.
COORDINATES: 25.32° N, 80.93° W.
TOTAL AREA: 1,508,537 acres.
ELEVATION RANGE: Sea level–8 ft.
ANNUAL VISITORS: Approx. 1 million.
OPERATING SEASON: Year-round; peak Nov.–Apr.
GOVERNING BODY: National Park Service.
MAIN ENTRANCES / GATEWAYS: Homestead, Shark Valley, and Gulf Coast at Everglades City.
PRIMARY LANDSCAPE TYPE: Subtropical wetlands and coastal estuaries.
MAJOR NATURAL LANDMARKS: Shark River Slough, Florida Bay, Ten Thousand Islands, and Anhinga Trail.
SIGNATURE WILDLIFE: American alligator, Florida panther, manatee, roseate spoonbill, and wood stork.
VEGETATION ZONES: Sawgrass prairie, mangrove forest, cypress dome, hardwood hammock, and coastal marsh.
CLIMATE: Humid subtropical with wet summers and mild, dry winters; average annual rainfall 60 in.
UNIQUE GEOLOGY / ECOSYSTEM: Vast slow-moving "River of Grass" flowing from Lake Okeechobee across limestone bedrock; largest tropical wilderness in the U.S.
INDIGENOUS HERITAGE: Inhabited for thousands of years by Calusa and Tequesta peoples who lived by fishing and shell gathering.
HISTORIC SIGNIFICANCE: Protected to preserve an ecosystem rather than scenery; recognized as a UNESCO World Heritage Site and International Biosphere Reserve.
FAMOUS LANDMARKS / TRAILS: Gumbo Limbo Trail, Mahogany Hammock, Flamingo Marina, and Shark Valley Observation Tower.
WHAT IT'S KNOWN FOR: Immense wetlands, unique hydrology, subtropical biodiversity, and rare species.
ACTIVITIES: Airboat tours, kayaking, birdwatching, photography, hiking, and wildlife viewing.
AVERAGE VISIT DURATION: 1–2 days.
VISITOR TIPS: Bring insect repellent, water, and sun protection; visit during the dry season for best wildlife viewing.
HIGHLIGHT: The Everglades' sawgrass marshes and winding waterways form America's most distinctive subtropical wilderness.

Cypress-lined waterways, Everglades National Park, Florida. Copyright © Lochlainn Seabrook.

GLACIER BAY NATIONAL PARK & PRESERVE

OFFICIAL NAME: Glacier Bay National Park and Preserve.
STATE: Alaska.
DESIGNATION: National Park and Preserve, established by act of Congress in 1980.
COORDINATES: 58°30 N, 137°0 W (approximate geographic centroid).
TOTAL AREA: Approximately 3,283,000 acres.
ELEVATION RANGE: Sea level–15,300 ft. on Mount Fairweather.
ANNUAL VISITORS: Around 700,000 annually.
OPERATING SEASON: Open year-round; peak visitation from late spring through early fall.
GOVERNING BODY: National Park Service.
MAIN ENTRANCES / GATEWAYS: Access by air or sea via Gustavus and Bartlett Cove.
PRIMARY LANDSCAPE TYPE: Glacial fjords, tidewater glaciers, coastal rainforest, and rugged peaks.
MAJOR NATURAL LANDMARKS: Margerie Glacier, Johns Hopkins Glacier, Tarr Inlet, and the Fairweather Range.
SIGNATURE WILDLIFE: Humpback whales, sea otters, brown bears, mountain goats, and bald eagles.
VEGETATION ZONES: Temperate rainforest, alpine tundra, and pioneer growth on glacial outwash.
CLIMATE: Maritime; cool, wet summers and mild winters with frequent precipitation.
UNIQUE GEOLOGY / ECOSYSTEM: Rapidly changing glacial landscape showcasing postglacial uplift and ecological succession.
INDIGENOUS HERITAGE: Homeland of the Huna Tlingit and Yakutat Tlingit, whose culture remains tied to the bay's waters.
HISTORIC SIGNIFICANCE: Noted for rapid glacial retreat and early scientific studies in glaciology and ecology.
FAMOUS LANDMARKS / TRAILS: Bartlett Cove Trail, Rainforest Trail, and boat excursions into Muir and Tarr Inlets.
WHAT IT'S KNOWN FOR: Towering tidewater glaciers, pristine fjords, and abundant marine life.
ACTIVITIES: Glacier viewing, kayaking, boating, wildlife watching, and photography.
AVERAGE VISIT DURATION: 1 day for cruise visitors; several days for backcountry exploration.
VISITOR TIPS: Dress for rain and cool temperatures; reserve access early; follow marine safety rules.
HIGHLIGHT: The 65-mile fjord system of Glacier Bay remains one of North America's grandest natural spectacles.

Johns Hopkins Glacier, Glacier Bay National Park and Preserve, Alaska. Copyright © Lochlainn Seabrook.

GLACIER NATIONAL PARK

OFFICIAL NAME: Glacier National Park.
STATE: Montana.
DESIGNATION: National Park; est. 1910.
COORDINATES: 48.6967° N, 113.7183° W.
TOTAL AREA: 1,013,128 acres.
ELEVATION RANGE: 3,150–10,466 ft. (Mount Cleveland).
ANNUAL VISITORS: About 3 million.
OPERATING SEASON: Open year-round; peak season June–September.
GOVERNING BODY: National Park Service.
MAIN ENTRANCES / GATEWAYS: West Glacier, St. Mary, Two Medicine, Many Glacier.
PRIMARY LANDSCAPE TYPE: Northern Rocky Mountain alpine and glacial valleys.
MAJOR NATURAL LANDMARKS: Going-to-the-Sun Road, Lake McDonald, Logan Pass, Grinnell Glacier, Many Glacier Valley.
SIGNATURE WILDLIFE: Grizzly bear, mountain goat, elk, moose, wolverine, bald eagle, and pika.
VEGETATION ZONES: Montane forests, subalpine meadows, alpine tundra, and riparian corridors rich in wildflowers.
CLIMATE: Continental mountain; long cold winters, cool wet springs, and short mild summers.
UNIQUE GEOLOGY / ECOSYSTEM: Precambrian Belt Supergroup rocks uplifted by the Lewis Overthrust; over 700 lakes, active glacial features, and the headwaters of three continental river systems.
INDIGENOUS HERITAGE: Homeland of the Blackfeet, Salish, and Kootenai Tribes, whose ancestral routes, seasonal camps, and sacred sites remain within the park.
HISTORIC SIGNIFICANCE: Known as the "Crown of the Continent," it preserves one of the largest intact ecosystems in the lower 48 states and is linked to early 20th-Century railway tourism.
WHAT IT'S KNOWN FOR: Towering peaks, turquoise lakes, wildflower meadows, and ancient glaciers that shaped the terrain.
ACTIVITIES: Hiking, photography, wildlife viewing, boating, camping, and scenic drives.
AVERAGE VISIT DURATION: 2–3 days.
VISITOR TIPS: Arrive early for parking, carry layers, and prepare for unpredictable weather even in midsummer.
HIGHLIGHT: The 67-mile Going-to-the-Sun Road offers breathtaking alpine vistas, abundant wildlife sightings, and unmatched access to the heart of the Northern Rockies.

Grinnell Point and Swiftcurrent Lake, Glacier National Park, Montana. Copyright © Lochlainn Seabrook.

GRAND CANYON NATIONAL PARK

OFFICIAL NAME: Grand Canyon National Park.
STATE: Arizona.
DESIGNATION: National Park; est. 1919.
COORDINATES: 36.1069° N, 112.1129° W.
TOTAL AREA: 1,217,262 acres.
ELEVATION RANGE: 1,200–9,200 ft.
ANNUAL VISITORS: Approx. 4.7 million.
OPERATING SEASON: All year. (A few remote sections remain closed to the public for safety/preservation/cultural reasons.
GOVERNING BODY: National Park Service.
MAIN ENTRANCES / GATEWAYS: South, East (Desert View), and North Rim entrances.
PRIMARY LANDSCAPE TYPE: Deep arid canyon carved by the Colorado River through layered sedimentary rock.
MAJOR NATURAL LANDMARKS: Colorado River, Bright Angel Canyon, Desert View Watchtower, and Vishnu Basin.
SIGNATURE WILDLIFE: Mule deer, elk, mountain lion, bighorn sheep, California condor, and Abert's squirrel.
VEGETATION ZONES: Desert scrub, pinyon-juniper woodland, ponderosa pine forest, and mixed conifer zones.
CLIMATE: Semi-arid; cold winters and hot, dry summers; large temperature differences between rim and inner canyon.
UNIQUE GEOLOGY / ECOSYSTEM: Exposes nearly 2 billion years of Earth's history in vividly stratified rock; supports desert, riparian, and alpine habitats.
INDIGENOUS HERITAGE: Homeland of Havasupai, Hopi, Navajo, Hualapai, and other Native peoples; numerous ancient dwellings and sacred sites.
HISTORIC SIGNIFICANCE: Recognized as a national treasure for its unmatched geological record and cultural importance.
FAMOUS LANDMARKS / TRAILS: Bright Angel Trail, South Kaibab Trail, North Kaibab Trail, Phantom Ranch, and Grand Canyon Village.
WHAT IT'S KNOWN FOR: Immense scale, multicolored cliffs, sweeping vistas, and the Colorado River's winding gorge.
ACTIVITIES: Hiking, photography, rafting, mule rides, scenic drives, camping, and ranger programs.
AVERAGE VISIT DURATION: 2–3 days.
VISITOR TIPS: Expect extreme temperature changes; bring water, sun protection, and layers; reserve lodging early.
HIGHLIGHT: Sunrise and sunset over the South Rim reveal brilliant hues across one of the planet's most spectacular wonders.

The South Rim of Grand Canyon National Park, Arizona, with the Colorado River visible below. Copyright © Lochlainn Seabrook.

GRAND TETON NATIONAL PARK

OFFICIAL NAME: Grand Teton National Park.
STATE: Wyoming.
DESIGNATION: National Park; est. 1929, expanded 1950.
COORDINATES: 43.7904° N, 110.6818° W.
TOTAL AREA: 310,044 acres.
ELEVATION RANGE: 6,320–13,775 ft.
ANNUAL VISITORS: About 3.4 million.
OPERATING SEASON: Year-round; peak May–Sept.
GOVERNING BODY: National Park Service.
MAIN ENTRANCES / GATEWAYS: Moose, Moran, and Granite Canyon Entrances; Jackson, WY.
PRIMARY LANDSCAPE TYPE: Alpine mountain range, glacial valleys, and sagebrush plains.
MAJOR NATURAL LANDMARKS: Teton Range, Snake River, Jenny Lake, and Jackson Lake.
SIGNATURE WILDLIFE: Elk, moose, bison, mule deer, grizzly and black bears, pronghorn, gray wolf, and bald eagle.
VEGETATION ZONES: Sagebrush flats, aspen groves, lodgepole pine forests, subalpine meadows, and alpine tundra.
CLIMATE: Cold winters, mild summers; avg. snowfall exceeds 400 in. in higher elevations.
UNIQUE GEOLOGY / ECOSYSTEM: Features a fault-block mountain range rising abruptly 7,000 ft. above the valley; active tectonic uplift with visible glacial features.
INDIGENOUS HERITAGE: Traditionally inhabited by Shoshone, Bannock, Crow, and other tribes for hunting and seasonal gathering.
HISTORIC SIGNIFICANCE: Early exploration by trappers and settlers shaped the region's frontier history; protected for its unmatched mountain scenery.
FAMOUS LANDMARKS / TRAILS: Cascade Canyon Trail, Jenny Lake Loop, Taggart Lake Trail, and Teton Crest Trail.
WHAT IT'S KNOWN FOR: Dramatic peaks, pristine alpine lakes, and iconic mountain vistas.
ACTIVITIES: Hiking, climbing, boating, wildlife viewing, and photography.
AVERAGE VISIT DURATION: 2–3 days.
VISITOR TIPS: Arrive early in summer; weather changes rapidly; bears frequent backcountry areas.
HIGHLIGHT: The Grand Teton, highest peak at 13,775 ft., dominates one of the most photographed landscapes in North America.

Jenny Lake and the Grand Teton Range, Grand Teton National Park, Wyoming. Copyright © Lochlainn Seabrook.

GREAT SAND DUNES NATIONAL PARK & PRESERVE

OFFICIAL NAME: Great Sand Dunes National Park and Preserve.
STATE: Colorado.
DESIGNATION: National Park and National Preserve; designated September 24, 2004.
COORDINATES: 37.75° N, 105.50° W.
TOTAL AREA: Approximately 149,000 acres.
ELEVATION RANGE: 7,520–13,604 ft.
ANNUAL VISITORS: About 512,000.
OPERATING SEASON: Open year-round, 24 hours daily.
GOVERNING BODY: National Park Service.
MAIN ENTRANCES / GATEWAYS: Access via State Highway 150 near Mosca, Colorado.
PRIMARY LANDSCAPE TYPE: High-elevation desert valley dune field flanked by alpine mountains.
MAJOR NATURAL LANDMARKS: Tallest dune field in North America and the Sangre de Cristo Mountains.
SIGNATURE WILDLIFE: Elk, pronghorn, mule deer, coyote, and Great Sand Dunes tiger beetle.
VEGETATION ZONES: Alpine tundra, subalpine forest, grasslands, shrublands, and wet sabkha zones.
CLIMATE: Semi-arid with warm days, cool nights, and cold winters; sand surface temperatures can exceed 150 °F in summer.
UNIQUE GEOLOGY / ECOSYSTEM: Wind- and water-driven dune system recycling ancient sand through mountain watersheds and creeks.
INDIGENOUS HERITAGE: Homeland of the Ute and Apache, occupied for over 9,000 years and still revered in tribal tradition.
HISTORIC SIGNIFICANCE: Protected as a national monument in 1932, later expanded to include the mountain and wetland ecosystems.
FAMOUS LANDMARKS / TRAILS: Star Dune, Medano Creek, Sand Ramp Trail, and Medano Pass Primitive Road.
WHAT IT'S KNOWN FOR: Towering golden dunes rising against snow-capped mountains in Colorado's San Luis Valley.
ACTIVITIES: Hiking, sand-sledding, creek play, stargazing, and backcountry camping.
AVERAGE VISIT DURATION: 1 day for the main dunes, 2 to 3 days for extended exploration.
VISITOR TIPS: Visit early or late to avoid heat, carry ample water, and check Medano Creek flow before arrival.
HIGHLIGHT: A vast expanse of shifting dunes and alpine peaks where silence, wind, and sunlight create an otherworldly landscape.

Sangre de Cristo Mountains, Great Sand Dunes National Park and Preserve, Colorado. Copyright © Lochlainn Seabrook.

GREAT SMOKY MOUNTAINS NATIONAL PARK

OFFICIAL NAME: Great Smoky Mountains National Park.
STATES: Tennessee and North Carolina.
DESIGNATION: National Park; est. 1934, dedicated 1940.
COORDINATES: 35.6118° N, 83.4895° W.
TOTAL AREA: 522,427 acres.
ELEVATION RANGE: 875–6,643 ft.
ANNUAL VISITORS: About 13 million.
OPERATING SEASON: Year-round.
GOVERNING BODY: National Park Service.
MAIN ENTRANCES / GATEWAYS: Gatlinburg, TN; Townsend, TN; Cherokee, NC.
PRIMARY LANDSCAPE TYPE: Southern Appalachian forested mountains.
MAJOR NATURAL LANDMARKS: Clingmans Dome, Cades Cove, Alum Cave Bluffs, Roaring Fork, Chimney Tops.
SIGNATURE WILDLIFE: Black bear, white-tailed deer, bobcat, wild turkey, salamanders, and river otters.
VEGETATION ZONES: Cove hardwood forest, spruce-fir, mixed oak-pine, and hemlock stands.
CLIMATE: Humid continental with cool, misty summers and mild, wet winters.
UNIQUE GEOLOGY / ECOSYSTEM: Composed of ancient Precambrian rocks and complex valleys carved by erosion; contains one of the most biodiverse temperate ecosystems on Earth.
INDIGENOUS HERITAGE: Homeland of the Cherokee Nation, who called the region Shaconage, "place of the blue smoke."
HISTORIC SIGNIFICANCE: Protected in 1934 to preserve the last large tract of Southern Appalachian wilderness after extensive logging and settlement clearing.
FAMOUS LANDMARKS / TRAILS: Appalachian Trail, Newfound Gap Road, Laurel Falls Trail, Chimney Tops Trail, Cades Cove Loop.
WHAT IT'S KNOWN FOR: Mist-covered peaks, rich biodiversity, and preserved pioneer homesteads that illustrate early mountain life.
ACTIVITIES: Hiking, camping, wildlife viewing, photography, auto touring, and horseback riding.
AVERAGE VISIT DURATION: 2–3 days.
VISITOR TIPS: Arrive early to avoid congestion; weather changes rapidly at higher elevations; fog can appear without warning.
HIGHLIGHT: From Clingmans Dome, the highest point in the park, panoramic views reveal wave after wave of smoky blue ridges fading to the horizon.

Great Smoky Mountains National Park, Tennessee and North Carolina. Copyright © Lochlainn Seabrook.

GUADALUPE MOUNTAINS NATIONAL PARK

OFFICIAL NAME: Guadalupe Mountains National Park.
STATE: Texas.
DESIGNATION: National Park; est. Sept. 30, 1972.
COORDINATES: 31.923° N, 104.868° W.
TOTAL AREA: 86,367 acres.
ELEVATION RANGE: 3,640–8,751 ft.
ANNUAL VISITORS: About 220,000.
OPERATING SEASON: Open year-round.
GOVERNING BODY: National Park Service.
MAIN ENTRANCES / GATEWAYS: Pine Springs, Dog Canyon, and McKittrick Canyon.
PRIMARY LANDSCAPE TYPE: Rugged desert mountains and canyons at the edge of the Chihuahuan Desert.
MAJOR NATURAL LANDMARKS: Guadalupe Peak, El Capitan, McKittrick Canyon, Salt Basin Dunes, and Williams Ranch.
SIGNATURE WILDLIFE: Mule deer, gray fox, black bear, mountain lion, golden eagle, and desert bighorn sheep.
VEGETATION ZONES: Chihuahuan Desert scrub, pinyon-juniper woodland, ponderosa pine forest, and high-country spruce-fir relics.
CLIMATE: Arid continental with hot summers, cold winters, and strong prevailing winds.
UNIQUE GEOLOGY / ECOSYSTEM: Contains the world's finest exposed Permian reef complex, the fossilized Capitan Reef, with dramatic limestone escarpments and cave systems.
INDIGENOUS HERITAGE: Once home to Mescalero Apache and earlier Jornada Mogollon peoples, who left pictographs and habitation sites.
HISTORIC SIGNIFICANCE: Served as a landmark on early frontier and Butterfield Overland Mail routes; ranching followed in the late 1800s.
FAMOUS LANDMARKS / TRAILS: Guadalupe Peak Trail, Devil's Hall Trail, McKittrick Canyon Trail, Smith Spring Loop.
WHAT IT'S KNOWN FOR: The highest point in Texas, vivid fall foliage, and preserved desert-mountain wilderness.
ACTIVITIES: Hiking, wildlife viewing, photography, backcountry camping, and geology study.
AVERAGE VISIT DURATION: 1–2 days.
VISITOR TIPS: Carry ample water, expect variable weather, and prepare for steep, exposed trails with limited shade.
HIGHLIGHT: Ascending Guadalupe Peak, "the Top of Texas," reveals sweeping views over the Chihuahuan Desert and the ancient Capitan Reef.

El Capitan, Guadalupe Mountains National Park, Texas. Copyright © Lochlainn Seabrook.

HALEAKALA NATIONAL PARK

OFFICIAL NAME: Haleakalā National Park.
STATE: Hawaii.
DESIGNATION: National Park; est. 1916.
COORDINATES: 20.72° N, 156.17° W.
TOTAL AREA: 33,265 acres.
ELEVATION RANGE: Sea level–10,023 ft.
ANNUAL VISITORS: Approximately 1 million.
OPERATING SEASON: Open year-round.
GOVERNING BODY: National Park Service.
MAIN ENTRANCES / GATEWAYS: Summit Entrance via Route 378; Kīpahulu District via Hana Highway.
PRIMARY LANDSCAPE TYPE: Volcanic highlands and coastal rainforest.
MAJOR NATURAL LANDMARKS: Haleakalā Crater, Puʻu ʻUlaʻula (Red Hill), Kīpahulu Valley, Waimoku Falls.
SIGNATURE WILDLIFE: Hawaiian goose (nēnē), Hawaiian petrel, Hawaiian hoary bat, native honeycreepers.
VEGETATION ZONES: Subalpine shrubland, montane forest, and coastal rainforest.
CLIMATE: Cool and dry at high elevations, warm and humid near sea level; temperatures range 40–80 °F.
UNIQUE GEOLOGY / ECOSYSTEM: Dominated by a massive dormant shield volcano with extensive lava flows, cinder cones, and one of the world's rarest alpine desert ecosystems.
INDIGENOUS HERITAGE: Sacred to Native Hawaiians; site of traditional ceremonies honoring ancient gods and goddesses.
HISTORIC SIGNIFICANCE: Incorporated from Hawaii National Park; preserves centuries of cultural sites, trails, and stone platforms.
FAMOUS LANDMARKS / TRAILS: Sliding Sands Trail, Halemauʻu Trail, Pipiwai Trail, Waimoku Falls Trail.
WHAT IT'S KNOWN FOR: Dramatic volcanic sunrise views, rare species, and striking contrasts between barren summit and lush coastal jungle.
ACTIVITIES: Hiking, bird-watching, photography, stargazing, ranger-led programs.
AVERAGE VISIT DURATION: 1–2 days.
VISITOR TIPS: Reserve sunrise entry early; pack warm layers and water; allow time for both summit and coastal districts.
HIGHLIGHT: Watching sunrise above the clouds from the 10,000-ft. summit of Haleakalā, where the horizon glows across a sea of mist and volcanic peaks.

Haleakala Crater, Haleakala National Park, Hawaii. Copyright © Lochlainn Seabrook.

HAWAI'I VOLCANOES NATIONAL PARK

OFFICIAL NAME: Hawai'i Volcanoes National Park.
STATE: Hawaii.
DESIGNATION: National Park; est. 1916.
COORDINATES: 19.4194° N, 155.2885° W.
TOTAL AREA: 523,000 acres.
ELEVATION RANGE: Sea level–13,681 ft.
ANNUAL VISITORS: Approx. 1.6 million.
OPERATING SEASON: Open year-round.
GOVERNING BODY: National Park Service.
MAIN ENTRANCES / GATEWAYS: Kīlauea Visitor Center via Highway 11; Kahuku Unit near Ocean View.
PRIMARY LANDSCAPE TYPE: Volcanic highlands, coastal lava plains, and rainforest slopes.
MAJOR NATURAL LANDMARKS: Kīlauea Caldera, Halema'uma'u Crater, Mauna Loa, Chain of Craters Road, Thurston Lava Tube.
SIGNATURE WILDLIFE: Hawaiian goose (nēnē), Hawaiian hoary bat, 'apapane, and endemic lava-adapted insects.
VEGETATION ZONES: Alpine shrubland, montane rainforest, lowland lava desert, and coastal grassland.
CLIMATE: Warm, humid tropics with strong elevation-based variation; heavy rainfall on windward slopes, dry leeward zones.
UNIQUE GEOLOGY / ECOSYSTEM: Contains two of Earth's most active volcanoes, ongoing lava flows, and rare primary succession habitats.
INDIGENOUS HERITAGE: Sacred homeland of Native Hawaiians; site of Pele worship and ancient trails linking villages to upland forests.
HISTORIC SIGNIFICANCE: Preserves centuries of Hawaiian habitation sites and one of the world's longest volcanic activity records.
FAMOUS LANDMARKS / TRAILS: Crater Rim Trail, Kīlauea Iki Trail, Devastation Trail, Pu'u Loa Petroglyphs, Mauna Loa Summit Trail.
WHAT IT'S KNOWN FOR: Ongoing volcanic eruptions, lava glow, steaming vents, and contrasts of fire and rainforest.
ACTIVITIES: Hiking, crater viewing, lava observation, bird-watching, photography, and ranger programs.
AVERAGE VISIT DURATION: 1–2 days.
VISITOR TIPS: Bring rain gear and layers; conditions shift quickly; check volcanic alerts before visiting.
HIGHLIGHT: Watching molten lava glow within Halema'uma'u Crater under a star-filled Hawaiian sky.

Halemaʻumaʻu Crater eruption, Hawaiʻi Volcanoes National Park, Hawaii. Copyright © Lochlainn Seabrook.

HOT SPRINGS NATIONAL PARK

OFFICIAL NAME: Hot Springs National Park.
STATE: Arkansas.
DESIGNATION: National Park; protected 1832, est. 1921.
COORDINATES: 34.521° N, 93.042° W.
TOTAL AREA: 5,550 acres.
ELEVATION RANGE: 575–1,405 ft.
ANNUAL VISITORS: About 2 million.
OPERATING SEASON: Open year-round.
GOVERNING BODY: National Park Service.
MAIN ENTRANCES / GATEWAYS: Central Ave., Hot Springs, Arkansas.
PRIMARY LANDSCAPE TYPE: Forested mountains and thermal springs.
MAJOR NATURAL LANDMARKS: Hot Springs Mountain, North Mountain, and 47 thermal springs.
SIGNATURE WILDLIFE: White-tailed deer, raccoon, gray fox, pileated woodpecker, and box turtle.
VEGETATION ZONES: Oak–hickory–pine forest typical of the Ouachita Mountains.
CLIMATE: Humid subtropical with hot summers, mild winters, and frequent rainfall.
UNIQUE GEOLOGY / ECOSYSTEM: Geothermal waters percolate deep underground, heating naturally before emerging at ~143 °F; one of the few non-volcanic thermal spring systems in the U.S.
INDIGENOUS HERITAGE: Long used by Indigenous peoples, including the Caddo and Quapaw, for ceremony and healing.
HISTORIC SIGNIFICANCE: Protected in 1832 as a federal reservation—predating Yellowstone—making it the earliest land set aside for public recreation and health.
FAMOUS LANDMARKS / TRAILS: Bathhouse Row, Grand Promenade, Goat Rock Trail, and Hot Springs Mountain Tower.
WHAT IT'S KNOWN FOR: Natural thermal springs, historic bathhouses, and scenic Ouachita landscapes.
ACTIVITIES: Bathing, hiking, birdwatching, scenic drives, and historical tours.
AVERAGE VISIT DURATION: 1–2 days.
VISITOR TIPS: Visit early to avoid parking congestion; bring water and sturdy shoes for steep trails.
HIGHLIGHT: The park's thermal waters have flowed continuously for thousands of years, forming the foundation of America's first health resort tradition.

Thermal pools, Hot Springs National Park, Arkansas. Copyright © Lochlainn Seabrook.

INDIANA DUNES NATIONAL PARK

OFFICIAL NAME: Indiana Dunes National Park.
STATE: Indiana.
DESIGNATION: National Park; est. February 15, 2019.
COORDINATES: 41.635° N, 87.058° W.
TOTAL AREA: 16,035 acres.
ELEVATION RANGE: From 597 ft. at lake level to nearly 900 ft. atop the highest dunes.
ANNUAL VISITORS: About 2.7 million annually.
OPERATING SEASON: Open year-round.
GOVERNING BODY: National Park Service.
MAIN ENTRANCES / GATEWAYS: Dorothy Buell Memorial Visitor Center in Porter; West Beach entrance via County Line Road.
PRIMARY LANDSCAPE TYPE: Lake-shore dunes, prairie, oak savanna, and wetlands.
MAJOR NATURAL LANDMARKS: Mount Baldy, Cowles Bog, Great Marsh, and the Little Calumet River.
SIGNATURE WILDLIFE: White-tailed deer, red fox, coyote, great blue heron, and migratory shorebirds.
VEGETATION ZONES: Dune grasses, oak-hickory forest, tallgrass prairie, and fen wetlands.
CLIMATE: Humid continental with warm summers, snowy winters, and strong lake-effect weather.
UNIQUE GEOLOGY / ECOSYSTEM: Formed by glacial retreat and lake-shore processes; features ridge-and-swale topography and high biological diversity.
HISTORIC SIGNIFICANCE: Protected through early 20th-Century conservation campaigns that preserved the dunes from industrial expansion and secured a refuge for native species and rare plants. The park remains a living classroom for ecological study and environmental restoration.
FAMOUS LANDMARKS / TRAILS: West Beach Succession Trail, Cowles Bog Trail, Little Calumet River Trail, Bailly Homestead.
WHAT IT'S KNOWN FOR: Towering sand dunes along Lake Michigan, exceptional biodiversity, and proximity to Chicago.
ACTIVITIES: Hiking, swimming, bird-watching, photography, and cross-country skiing.
AVERAGE VISIT DURATION: Typically 3–5 hours; overnight visitors often stay 1–2 days.
HIGHLIGHT: The park's ever-shifting dunes and rare ecosystems create a living landscape where Great Lakes wilderness meets urban America.

Sand dunes overlooking Lake Michigan Indiana Dunes National Park, Indiana. Copyright © Lochlainn Seabrook.

ISLE ROYALE NATIONAL PARK

OFFICIAL NAME: Isle Royale National Park.
STATE: Michigan.
DESIGNATION: National Park; est. April 3, 1940.
COORDINATES: 48°06 N, 88°30 W.
TOTAL AREA: Approximately 571,790 acres, including 132,018 acres of land.
ELEVATION RANGE: 600 ft. at Lake Superior to 1,394 ft. at Mount Desor.
ANNUAL VISITORS: Around 28,800 per year.
OPERATING SEASON: Open mid-April through October; closed in winter.
GOVERNING BODY: National Park Service.
MAIN ENTRANCES / GATEWAYS: Access by ferry or seaplane from Houghton and Copper Harbor, Michigan.
PRIMARY LANDSCAPE TYPE: Remote archipelago of forested ridges, lakes, and rocky shoreline within Lake Superior.
MAJOR NATURAL LANDMARKS: Greenstone Ridge, Mount Desor, Siskiwit Lake, and numerous glacial bays.
SIGNATURE WILDLIFE: Moose, gray wolves, beavers, red foxes, and common loons.
VEGETATION ZONES: Boreal and northern hardwood forests of spruce, fir, birch, and maple with open ridges and bogs.
CLIMATE: Short cool summers, long cold winters, and frequent fog from Lake Superior.
UNIQUE GEOLOGY / ECOSYSTEM: Ancient lava flows and glacially carved ridges forming a rare island ecosystem with over 400 islets.
INDIGENOUS HERITAGE: Ojibwe and earlier Native peoples mined native copper and fished here for thousands of years.
HISTORIC SIGNIFICANCE: Protected for its isolation and intact wilderness; named an International Biosphere Reserve in 1980.
FAMOUS LANDMARKS / TRAILS: Greenstone Ridge Trail, Island Mine Trail, and Feldtmann Ridge Trail.
WHAT IT'S KNOWN FOR: Its remote beauty, wolf-moose study, and complete absence of roads or cars.
ACTIVITIES: Backpacking, canoeing, kayaking, fishing, diving, and wildlife viewing.
AVERAGE VISIT DURATION: 2–4 days for most visitors.
VISITOR TIPS: Plan transport early, pack light but well, and prepare for sudden weather shifts.
HIGHLIGHT: A solitary wilderness in Lake Superior offering one of America's most untouched and self-reliant park experiences.

Isle Royale National Park, Michigan. Copyright © Lochlainn Seabrook.

JOSHUA TREE NATIONAL PARK

OFFICIAL NAME: Joshua Tree National Park.
STATE: California.
DESIGNATION: National Park; designated 1936, est. 1994.
COORDINATES: 33.8734° N, 115.9010° W.
TOTAL AREA: 795,156 acres.
ELEVATION RANGE: 536–5,814 ft.
ANNUAL VISITORS: Approx. 3 million.
OPERATING SEASON: Year-round; peak visitation October–May.
GOVERNING BODY: National Park Service.
MAIN ENTRANCES / GATEWAYS: West Entrance (Joshua Tree), North Entrance (Twentynine Palms), South Entrance (Cottonwood).
PRIMARY LANDSCAPE TYPE: High and low desert basins divided by rugged mountains.
MAJOR NATURAL LANDMARKS: Keys View, Hidden Valley, Skull Rock, Barker Dam, Cholla Cactus Garden.
SIGNATURE WILDLIFE: Desert bighorn sheep, jackrabbit, coyote, desert tortoise, roadrunner.
VEGETATION ZONES: Mojave Desert (Joshua tree woodlands) and Colorado Desert (creosote bush scrub).
CLIMATE: Hot, arid summers; cool winters; average annual rainfall under 6 in.
UNIQUE GEOLOGY / ECOSYSTEM: Known for monzogranite formations and the meeting of two desert ecosystems rich in biodiversity.
INDIGENOUS HERITAGE: Inhabited for millennia by Cahuilla, Serrano, and Chemehuevi peoples who left petroglyphs and habitation sites.
HISTORIC SIGNIFICANCE: Designated a national monument in 1936 for its desert ecology and later protected as wilderness.
FAMOUS LANDMARKS / TRAILS: Hidden Valley Trail, Barker Dam Trail, Ryan Mountain, Keys Ranch.
WHAT IT'S KNOWN FOR: Iconic Joshua trees, rock climbing, and vast desert vistas.
ACTIVITIES: Hiking, climbing, camping, birding, stargazing, photography.
AVERAGE VISIT DURATION: 1–3 days.
VISITOR TIPS: Bring ample water, avoid midday hikes, and check weather advisories.
HIGHLIGHT: At sunset the granite peaks and Joshua trees glow gold against violet desert skies.

Joshua trees (*Yucca brevifolia*), Joshua Tree National Park, California. Copyright © Lochlainn Seabrook.

KENAI FJORDS NATIONAL PARK

OFFICIAL NAME: Kenai Fjords National Park.
STATE: Alaska.
DESIGNATION: National Park; est. 1980.
COORDINATES: 59.92° N, 149.65° W.
TOTAL AREA: 669,983 acres.
ELEVATION RANGE: Sea level–6,612 ft.
ANNUAL VISITORS: About 400,000.
OPERATING SEASON: Year-round; main access May–Sept.
GOVERNING BODY: National Park Service.
MAIN ENTRANCES / GATEWAYS: Seward and Exit Glacier Road.
PRIMARY LANDSCAPE TYPE: Coastal fjords, glaciers, icefields, and rugged mountain ridges.
MAJOR NATURAL LANDMARKS: Harding Icefield, Exit Glacier, Aialik Bay, Nuka Bay, and Holgate Arm.
SIGNATURE WILDLIFE: Sea otters, harbor seals, Steller sea lions, black bears, mountain goats, puffins, humpback and orca whales.
VEGETATION ZONES: Coastal spruce-hemlock forest, alpine tundra, glacier forelands, and wet meadows.
CLIMATE: Maritime subarctic; cool, wet summers and snowy, stormy winters.
UNIQUE GEOLOGY / ECOSYSTEM: Formed by intense glacial erosion; contains tidewater glaciers, fjords over 900 ft. deep, and dynamic icefield ecosystems supporting both marine and terrestrial life.
INDIGENOUS HERITAGE: Traditionally inhabited by the Alutiiq (Sugpiaq) people who hunted marine mammals, fished, and navigated the fjords for trade.
HISTORIC SIGNIFICANCE: Protects one of North America's largest remaining icefields and provides vital research on glacial retreat and climate change.
FAMOUS LANDMARKS / TRAILS: Harding Icefield Trail, Exit Glacier Overlook, Aialik Bay kayak routes, and Holgate Arm.
WHAT IT'S KNOWN FOR: Towering glaciers descending into the sea, diverse marine life, and dramatic coastal wilderness.
ACTIVITIES: Kayaking, glacier trekking, boating, wildlife cruises, hiking, and photography.
AVERAGE VISIT DURATION: 1–2 days.
VISITOR TIPS: Dress for cold, wet weather; boat tours and guided hikes offer the best glacier and wildlife views.
HIGHLIGHT: Watching massive tidewater glaciers calve into deep blue fjords surrounded by whales and seabirds.

Harding Icefield, Kenai Fjords National Park, Alaska. Copyright © Lochlainn Seabrook.

LASSEN VOLCANIC NATIONAL PARK

OFFICIAL NAME: Lassen Volcanic National Park.
STATE: California.
DESIGNATION: National Park; est. August 9, 1916.
COORDINATES: 40.49° N, 121.51° W.
TOTAL AREA: 106,452 acres.
ELEVATION RANGE: 5,650–10,457 ft.
ANNUAL VISITORS: About 500,000.
OPERATING SEASON: Year-round; main access roads open roughly May–Oct.
GOVERNING BODY: National Park Service.
MAIN ENTRANCES / GATEWAYS: Southwest Entrance near Mineral; Northwest Entrance via Manzanita Lake.
PRIMARY LANDSCAPE TYPE: Volcanic peaks, alpine lakes, meadows, and conifer forests.
MAJOR NATURAL LANDMARKS: Lassen Peak, Bumpass Hell, Manzanita Lake, and Chaos Crags.
SIGNATURE WILDLIFE: Black bear, mule deer, pine marten, mountain lion, and bald eagle.
VEGETATION ZONES: Mixed conifer forest, red fir forest, subalpine woodland, and alpine tundra.
CLIMATE: Cold snowy winters; mild dry summers; high elevation produces large temperature swings.
UNIQUE GEOLOGY / ECOSYSTEM: Contains all four major volcanic types—shield, plug dome, cinder cone, and stratovolcano—within one park; active hydrothermal areas persist.
INDIGENOUS HERITAGE: Homeland of the Atsugewi, Yana, and Maidu peoples, who hunted, fished, and gathered along mountain slopes and lakes.
HISTORIC SIGNIFICANCE: Site of Lassen Peak eruptions from 1914–1917; proclaimed national park in 1916 to preserve active volcanic landscapes.
FAMOUS LANDMARKS / TRAILS: Bumpass Hell Trail, Lassen Peak Trail, Manzanita Lake Loop, Cinder Cone Trail.
WHAT IT'S KNOWN FOR: Active geothermal features, snow-capped volcanic summits, pristine alpine scenery, and solitude.
ACTIVITIES: Hiking, photography, camping, snowshoeing, cross-country skiing, and geology observation.
AVERAGE VISIT DURATION: 1–2 days.
VISITOR TIPS: Check road closures before arrival; summer offers best access; pack layers for rapidly changing weather.
HIGHLIGHT: Standing atop Lassen Peak reveals panoramic views of the southern Cascades and the park's living volcanic terrain.

Lassen Peak overlooking Manzanita Lake, Lassen Volcanic National Park, California. Copyright © Lochlainn Seabrook.

MAMMOTH CAVE NATIONAL PARK

OFFICIAL NAME: Mammoth Cave National Park.
STATE: Kentucky.
DESIGNATION: National Park; est. 1941; UNESCO World Heritage Site 1981.
COORDINATES: 37.186° N, 86.101° W.
TOTAL AREA: 52,830 acres.
ELEVATION RANGE: 433–886 ft.
ANNUAL VISITORS: Approx. 2 million.
OPERATING SEASON: Open year-round; tours vary seasonally.
GOVERNING BODY: National Park Service.
MAIN ENTRANCES / GATEWAYS: Park City; Cave City; Brownsville.
PRIMARY LANDSCAPE TYPE: Karst plateau with sinkholes, ridges, and river valleys.
MAJOR NATURAL LANDMARKS: Mammoth Cave system; Green River; Echo River; Cedar Sink.
SIGNATURE WILDLIFE: Bats, white-tailed deer, raccoons, salamanders, cave crickets, and cave shrimp.
VEGETATION ZONES: Oak-hickory forests, mixed hardwoods, riparian zones, and cave mosses.
CLIMATE: Humid subtropical; warm summers, mild winters, steady rainfall year-round.
UNIQUE GEOLOGY / ECOSYSTEM: World's longest known cave system—over 426 miles explored—formed in Mississippian limestone beneath sandstone caprock.
INDIGENOUS HERITAGE: Inhabited by Native Americans over 5,000 years ago; artifacts show mining, burial, and ceremonial use.
HISTORIC SIGNIFICANCE: Site of 19th-Century saltpeter mining and one of America's earliest tourist destinations.
FAMOUS LANDMARKS / TRAILS: Historic Entrance; Frozen Niagara; Gothic Avenue; Green River Bluffs Trail; Cedar Sink Trail.
WHAT IT'S KNOWN FOR: Vast subterranean passages, underground rivers, rare troglobitic species, and rich archaeological record.
ACTIVITIES: Cave tours, hiking, camping, canoeing, birding, and photography.
AVERAGE VISIT DURATION: 1–2 days.
VISITOR TIPS: Reserve tours early; bring layers for cool underground temperatures (~54 °F year-round).
HIGHLIGHT: The Historic Tour reveals towering chambers, flowstone formations, and ancient saltpeter vats deep within the world's largest cave system.

Entrance passage, Mammoth Cave National Park, Kentucky. Copyright © Lochlainn Seabrook.

MESA VERDE NATIONAL PARK

OFFICIAL NAME: Mesa Verde National Park.
STATE: Colorado.
DESIGNATION: National Park; est. 1906; UNESCO World Heritage Site 1978.
COORDINATES: 37.18° N, 108.49° W.
TOTAL AREA: 52,485 acres.
ELEVATION RANGE: 6,000–8,572 ft.
ANNUAL VISITORS: About 600,000.
OPERATING SEASON: Year-round; peak months May–Oct.
GOVERNING BODY: National Park Service.
MAIN ENTRANCES / GATEWAYS: Near Cortez and Mancos via U.S. 160.
PRIMARY LANDSCAPE TYPE: High-desert plateau with deep sandstone canyons.
MAJOR NATURAL LANDMARKS: Chapin Mesa, Cliff Canyon, Balcony House, and Soda Canyon.
SIGNATURE WILDLIFE: Mule deer, elk, black bear, gray fox, and golden eagle.
VEGETATION ZONES: Pinyon-juniper woodland, sagebrush, ponderosa pine, and Gambel oak.
CLIMATE: Semi-arid; warm summers, cold snowy winters; 18 in. annual precipitation.
UNIQUE GEOLOGY / ECOSYSTEM: Late Cretaceous sandstones and shales forming mesas eroded by the Mancos River; supports diverse high-desert flora and fauna.
INDIGENOUS HERITAGE: Home to Ancestral Puebloans from roughly A.D. 550–1300; over 4,700 recorded archaeological sites.
HISTORIC SIGNIFICANCE: Preserves some of North America's finest ancient cliff dwellings, revealing advanced pre-Columbian engineering and agriculture.
FAMOUS LANDMARKS / TRAILS: Cliff Palace, Spruce Tree House, Balcony House, Petroglyph Point Trail.
WHAT IT'S KNOWN FOR: Exceptional cliff dwellings and cultural continuity linking ancient Pueblo peoples to modern tribes.
ACTIVITIES: Guided tours, hiking, scenic drives, photography, and archaeological study.
AVERAGE VISIT DURATION: 1–2 days.
VISITOR TIPS: Reserve ranger-led tours early; limited access to some dwellings; carry water and sun protection.
HIGHLIGHT: Cliff Palace—largest cliff dwelling in North America, featuring 150 rooms and 23 kivas carved into sandstone; a masterwork of ancient Southwestern architecture.

Cliff Palace, Mesa Verde National Park, Colorado. Copyright © Lochlainn Seabrook.

MOUNT RAINIER NATIONAL PARK

OFFICIAL NAME: Mount Rainier National Park.
STATE: Washington.
DESIGNATION: National Park; est. 1899.
COORDINATES: 46.85° N, 121.76° W.
TOTAL AREA: 236,381 acres.
ELEVATION RANGE: 1,600–14,410 ft.
ANNUAL VISITORS: Approx. 1.6 million.
OPERATING SEASON: Year-round; peak access June–September.
GOVERNING BODY: National Park Service.
MAIN ENTRANCES / GATEWAYS: Nisqually, Carbon River, White River, and Stevens Canyon.
PRIMARY LANDSCAPE TYPE: Stratovolcano, alpine glaciers, subalpine meadows, and dense conifer forests.
MAJOR NATURAL LANDMARKS: Mount Rainier, Paradise, Sunrise, Carbon Glacier, and Narada Falls.
SIGNATURE WILDLIFE: Black bears, elk, mountain goats, marmots, pikas, and northern spotted owls.
VEGETATION ZONES: Temperate rain forest, montane fir-hemlock forest, subalpine meadows, and alpine tundra.
CLIMATE: Maritime with cool, wet winters and mild, dry summers; heavy snowfall at higher elevations.
UNIQUE GEOLOGY / ECOSYSTEM: Active stratovolcano rising above the Cascade Range with more glacial ice than any other U.S. peak outside Alaska; source of five major rivers.
INDIGENOUS HERITAGE: Homeland of the Puyallup, Nisqually, Muckleshoot, Yakama, and Cowlitz peoples who used the mountain's slopes for hunting and spiritual ceremonies.
HISTORIC SIGNIFICANCE: Fifth national park created; early mountaineering and glacier research center; model for wilderness preservation in the Pacific Northwest.
FAMOUS LANDMARKS / TRAILS: Wonderland Trail, Skyline Trail, Paradise Valley, Reflection Lakes, Grove of the Patriarchs.
WHAT IT'S KNOWN FOR: The tallest volcano in the contiguous U.S., vast glaciers, and spectacular wildflower meadows.
ACTIVITIES: Hiking, climbing, camping, snowshoeing, and photography.
AVERAGE VISIT DURATION: 1–3 days.
VISITOR TIPS: Weather changes rapidly; carry layers and check road conditions before entry.
HIGHLIGHT: The 93-mile Wonderland Trail encircles Mount Rainier through glaciers, waterfalls, alpine wildflower basins, and old-growth forests.

Paradise Meadows, Mount Rainier National Park, Washington. Copyright © Lochlainn Seabrook.

NORTH CASCADES NATIONAL PARK

OFFICIAL NAME: North Cascades National Park.
STATE: Washington.
DESIGNATION: National Park; est. October 2, 1968.
COORDINATES: 48°30 N, 121°00 W.
TOTAL AREA: 504,654 acres.
ELEVATION RANGE: 400–9,220 ft. (Goode Mountain).
ANNUAL VISITORS: Approximately 16,000.
OPERATING SEASON: Open year-round; most roads close November–May due to snow.
GOVERNING BODY: National Park Service.
MAIN ENTRANCES / GATEWAYS: State Route 20 via Newhalem and Marblemount; Stehekin via Lake Chelan ferry.
PRIMARY LANDSCAPE TYPE: Glaciated mountain wilderness with deep valleys and dense conifer forests.
MAJOR NATURAL LANDMARKS: Picket Range, Cascade Pass, Goode Mountain, Ross Lake, Diablo Lake.
SIGNATURE WILDLIFE: Mountain goats, black bears, wolverines, marmots, peregrine falcons.
VEGETATION ZONES: Coastal rainforest to alpine tundra across eight life zones.
CLIMATE: Maritime west side wet and snowy; east side dry and sunny; heavy snowpack at high elevations.
UNIQUE GEOLOGY / ECOSYSTEM: Formed by accreted terranes and Pleistocene glaciation; contains over 300 active glaciers.
INDIGENOUS HERITAGE: Homeland of Upper Skagit, Sauk-Suiattle, and Nooksack Tribes; longstanding salmon and mountain resource use.
HISTORIC SIGNIFICANCE: Remote area of mining and hydroelectric exploration before protection in 1968 as a wilderness park.
FAMOUS LANDMARKS / TRAILS: Cascade Pass Trail, Thunder Creek Trail, Stehekin Valley, Picket Range Traverse.
WHAT IT'S KNOWN FOR: Sheer relief, hundreds of glaciers, and one of the most untouched mountain ecosystems in the Lower 48.
ACTIVITIES: Hiking, mountaineering, backpacking, boating, wildlife viewing.
AVERAGE VISIT DURATION: 1–3 days; longer for backcountry travel.
VISITOR TIPS: Verify SR-20 status, secure permits, and prepare for rapid weather changes and limited services.
HIGHLIGHT: A vast and rugged alpine wilderness where jagged peaks and active glaciers preserve the wild center of the Cascades.

Diablo Lake, North Cascades National Park, Washington. Copyright © Lochlainn Seabrook.

OLYMPIC NATIONAL PARK

OFFICIAL NAME: Olympic National Park.
STATE: Washington.
DESIGNATION: National Park; est. 1938.
COORDINATES: 47.97° N, 123.50° W.
TOTAL AREA: 922,650 acres.
ELEVATION RANGE: Sea level–7,980 ft. at Mount Olympus.
ANNUAL VISITORS: About 2.4 million.
OPERATING SEASON: Open year-round, though high-elevation areas close in winter.
GOVERNING BODY: National Park Service.
MAIN ENTRANCES / GATEWAYS: Port Angeles, Quinault, and Hoh Rain Forest entrances.
PRIMARY LANDSCAPE TYPE: Coastal wilderness, temperate rain forest, alpine peaks, and river valleys.
MAJOR NATURAL LANDMARKS: Mount Olympus, Hoh Rain Forest, Hurricane Ridge, and Rialto Beach.
SIGNATURE WILDLIFE: Roosevelt elk, black bear, mountain goat, bald eagle, and river otter.
VEGETATION ZONES: Coastal Sitka spruce, lowland western hemlock, montane fir, and alpine meadows.
CLIMATE: Maritime with heavy precipitation along the west; snow in high elevations, mild summers.
UNIQUE GEOLOGY / ECOSYSTEM: Glaciated peaks, basalt sea stacks, and old-growth rain forests hosting diverse endemic species.
INDIGENOUS HERITAGE: Traditionally inhabited by the Hoh, Quinault, Makah, Quileute, and Klallam peoples whose cultures remain tied to the land and sea.
HISTORIC SIGNIFICANCE: Preserved as a wilderness refuge for ancient rain forests and native wildlife; designated a UNESCO World Heritage Site in 1981.
FAMOUS LANDMARKS / TRAILS: Hoh River Trail, Hurricane Ridge, Sol Duc Hot Springs, and Rialto Beach.
WHAT IT'S KNOWN FOR: Vast ecological diversity, lush rain forests, and glacier-clad mountains within a single park.
ACTIVITIES: Hiking, backpacking, wildlife viewing, tidepooling, kayaking, camping, and mountaineering.
AVERAGE VISIT DURATION: 2–4 days.
VISITOR TIPS: Prepare for rapid weather changes and bring rain gear even in summer; coastal fog can appear suddenly.
HIGHLIGHT: A living museum of coastal, forest, and alpine ecosystems in one of America's wildest and most pristine natural sanctuaries.

Rialto Beach, Olympic National Park, Washington. Copyright © Lochlainn Seabrook.

PETRIFIED FOREST NATIONAL PARK

OFFICIAL NAME: Petrified Forest National Park.
STATE: Arizona.
DESIGNATION: National Park; monument 1906, est. 1962.
COORDINATES: 34.95° N, 109.78° W.
TOTAL AREA: 221,390 acres.
ELEVATION RANGE: 5,340–6,230 ft.
ANNUAL VISITORS: About 500,000.
OPERATING SEASON: Year-round; closed Dec. 25.
GOVERNING BODY: National Park Service.
MAIN ENTRANCES / GATEWAYS: I-40 north; U.S. 180 south near Holbrook.
PRIMARY LANDSCAPE TYPE: Painted Desert badlands, open grasslands, and fossil woodlands.
MAJOR NATURAL LANDMARKS: Rainbow Forest, Blue Mesa, Crystal Forest, Pilot Rock.
SIGNATURE WILDLIFE: Pronghorns, coyotes, bobcats, jackrabbits, horned lizards.
VEGETATION ZONES: Shortgrass steppe with sagebrush, rabbitbrush, junipers, and yucca.
CLIMATE: Cold semi-arid; hot dry summers, freezing nights, brief summer monsoon.
UNIQUE GEOLOGY / ECOSYSTEM: Late Triassic Chinle Formation containing vast petrified-wood beds, fossilized ferns, and bones of early reptiles and amphibians.
INDIGENOUS HERITAGE: Once home to Ancestral Puebloan peoples who built stone dwellings and carved petroglyphs across the mesas.
HISTORIC SIGNIFICANCE: Among the first fossil regions preserved for science; traversed by historic Route 66 and the Santa Fe rail line.
FAMOUS LANDMARKS / TRAILS: Giant Logs Trail, Blue Mesa Loop, Agate House, Painted Desert Rim Trail.
WHAT IT'S KNOWN FOR: Multicolored badlands and ancient trees turned to quartz crystal over 200 million years ago.
ACTIVITIES: Scenic drives, short hikes, fossil exhibits, wilderness treks, photography, and geologic study.
AVERAGE VISIT DURATION: 2–4 hours.
VISITOR TIPS: Best light early or late; watch summer storms from overlooks; carry water and sun gear.
HIGHLIGHT: A Triassic forest transformed into shimmering stone within Arizona's vivid Painted Desert, where prehistory joins up with the modern Southwest.

Petrified logs, Petrified Forest National Park, Arizona. Copyright © Lochlainn Seabrook.

REDWOOD NATIONAL & STATE PARKS

OFFICIAL NAME: Redwood National and State Parks.
STATE: California.
DESIGNATION: National and State Parks; est. 1968.
COORDINATES: 41.2132° N, 124.0046° W.
TOTAL AREA: 138,999 acres.
ELEVATION RANGE: Sea level–3,170 ft.
ANNUAL VISITORS: About 450,000.
OPERATING SEASON: Open year-round.
GOVERNING BODY: National Park Service and California State Parks.
MAIN ENTRANCES / GATEWAYS: Crescent City, Klamath, Orick, and Trinidad.
PRIMARY LANDSCAPE TYPE: Coastal temperate rainforest, rivers, and Pacific shoreline.
MAJOR NATURAL LANDMARKS: Tall Trees Grove, Lady Bird Johnson Grove, Redwood Creek, and Gold Bluffs Beach.
SIGNATURE WILDLIFE: Roosevelt elk, black bear, bobcat, river otter, gray whale, bald eagle, and marbled murrelet.
VEGETATION ZONES: Coast redwood forests, Sitka spruce groves, oak woodlands, and coastal prairies.
CLIMATE: Cool marine climate with mild winters, foggy summers, and 100 in. annual rainfall.
UNIQUE GEOLOGY / ECOSYSTEM: Part of the Klamath-Siskiyou bioregion with active coastal uplift and nutrient-rich soils supporting towering redwoods over 350 ft. tall.
INDIGENOUS HERITAGE: Homeland of the Tolowa, Yurok, and Chilula peoples who harvested salmon for food and redwood for canoes and ceremonial objects.
HISTORIC SIGNIFICANCE: Logging in the 1800s destroyed most old-growth forests; preservation began in the 1920s and the federal park was created in 1968 to protect the last stands.
FAMOUS LANDMARKS / TRAILS: Newton B. Drury Scenic Parkway, Redwood Creek Trail, Fern Canyon, Prairie Creek Trail.
WHAT IT'S KNOWN FOR: World's tallest trees and one of the most diverse temperate rainforests on Earth.
ACTIVITIES: Hiking, wildlife viewing, scenic drives, camping, and beachcombing.
AVERAGE VISIT DURATION: 1–2 days.
VISITOR TIPS: Expect heavy fog and wet conditions; dress in layers and bring waterproof gear.
HIGHLIGHT: Standing among centuries-old redwoods rising over 30 stories is an awe-inspiring encounter with Earth's ancient living giants.

Redwoods (*Sequoia sempervirens*), Redwood National and State Parks, California. Copyright © Lochlainn Seabrook.

ROCKY MOUNTAIN NATIONAL PARK

OFFICIAL NAME: Rocky Mountain National Park.
STATE: Colorado.
DESIGNATION: National Park; est. January 26, 1915.
COORDINATES: 40.4° N, 105.6° W.
TOTAL AREA: 265,847 acres.
ELEVATION RANGE: 7,860–14,259 ft.
ANNUAL VISITORS: Approximately 4.4 million.
OPERATING SEASON: Open year-round; high-elevation roads close seasonally due to snow.
GOVERNING BODY: National Park Service.
MAIN ENTRANCES / GATEWAYS: Beaver Meadows and Fall River near Estes Park; Grand Lake on the west side.
PRIMARY LANDSCAPE TYPE: Alpine and subalpine mountain wilderness with valleys, forests, lakes, and tundra.
MAJOR NATURAL LANDMARKS: Longs Peak, Trail Ridge Road, Bear Lake, and the Continental Divide.
SIGNATURE WILDLIFE: Elk, mule deer, moose, black bear, bighorn sheep, coyote, marmot, and pika.
VEGETATION ZONES: Montane forests of ponderosa pine; subalpine spruce-fir; alpine tundra above tree line.
CLIMATE: Cool, dry, and variable; summer highs near 70 °F in valleys and freezing temperatures year-round at higher elevations.
UNIQUE GEOLOGY / ECOSYSTEM: Precambrian granites and schists shaped by glaciation; supports diverse alpine and montane ecosystems.
INDIGENOUS HERITAGE: Long used by Ute and Arapaho peoples for hunting, travel, and spiritual purposes.
HISTORIC SIGNIFICANCE: Preserves one of America's most accessible high-mountain environments for study and recreation.
FAMOUS LANDMARKS / TRAILS: Trail Ridge Road, Longs Peak Trail, Bear Lake Trail, and Moraine Park.
WHAT IT'S KNOWN FOR: Towering peaks, sweeping tundra vistas, abundant wildlife, and the highest continuous paved road in the nation.
ACTIVITIES: Hiking, scenic drives, photography, camping, wildlife viewing, and snowshoeing.
AVERAGE VISIT DURATION: 4 hours to several days depending on route, elevation, and weather conditions.
VISITOR TIPS: Expect rapid weather changes; carry layers, water, and sun protection; arrive early in peak months.
HIGHLIGHT: The view from Trail Ridge Road reveals a seamless panorama of alpine tundra stretching above the Continental Divide, unmatched in the Rockies.

Longs Peak, Rocky Mountain National Park, Colorado. Copyright © Lochlainn Seabrook.

SAGUARO NATIONAL PARK

OFFICIAL NAME: Saguaro National Park.
STATE: Arizona.
DESIGNATION: National Park; protected 1933; est. 1994.
COORDINATES: 32.25° N, 110.50° W.
TOTAL AREA: 91,716 acres.
ELEVATION RANGE: 2,180–8,666 ft.
ANNUAL VISITORS: About 1 million.
OPERATING SEASON: Open year-round; best months Nov.–Apr.
GOVERNING BODY: National Park Service.
MAIN ENTRANCES / GATEWAYS: Tucson Mountain District (west) and Rincon Mountain District (east), near Tucson.
PRIMARY LANDSCAPE TYPE: Sonoran Desert with rugged mountain ranges.
MAJOR NATURAL LANDMARKS: Rincon Mountains, Tanque Verde Ridge, Wasson Peak, Cactus Forest Drive.
SIGNATURE WILDLIFE: Desert tortoise, Gila monster, coyote, javelina, mule deer, Harris' hawk.
VEGETATION ZONES: Desert scrub, foothill grasslands, oak woodland, pine–fir forest at higher elevations.
CLIMATE: Hot, dry desert climate; summer highs often exceed 100 °F; winter mild and sunny.
UNIQUE GEOLOGY / ECOSYSTEM: Characterized by granitic and volcanic formations, bajadas, and alluvial fans supporting the world's densest stands of giant saguaro cacti.
INDIGENOUS HERITAGE: Homeland of the Tohono O'odham people, who view the saguaro as a sacred ancestor and harvest its fruit in traditional ceremonies.
HISTORIC SIGNIFICANCE: Protected since 1933 to preserve the emblematic saguaro and desert ecosystem of southern Arizona.
FAMOUS LANDMARKS / TRAILS: Cactus Forest Trail, King Canyon Trail, Wasson Peak Trail, Tanque Verde Ridge Trail.
WHAT IT'S KNOWN FOR: Towering saguaro forests, vivid sunsets, and vast desert panoramas framed by distant mountains.
ACTIVITIES: Scenic drives, hiking, photography, birdwatching, wildflower viewing, stargazing, and desert ecology study.
AVERAGE VISIT DURATION: 3–5 hours.
VISITOR TIPS: Bring ample water, sun protection, and start hikes early; no services within park boundaries; watch for monsoon storms in summer.
HIGHLIGHT: Home to North America's largest cactus—the saguaro—which can reach 50 ft. tall and live over 150 years.

Saguaro cacti (*Carnegiea gigantea*), Saguaro National Park, Arizona. Copyright © Lochlainn Seabrook.

SEQUOIA NATIONAL PARK

OFFICIAL NAME: Sequoia National Park.
STATE: California.
DESIGNATION: National Park; est. 1890.
COORDINATES: 36.4864° N, 118.5658° W.
TOTAL AREA: 404,064 acres.
ELEVATION RANGE: 1,370–14,494 ft.
ANNUAL VISITORS: About 1 million.
OPERATING SEASON: Year-round, with limited winter access.
GOVERNING BODY: National Park Service.
MAIN ENTRANCES / GATEWAYS: Ash Mountain near Three Rivers and Foothills near Visalia.
PRIMARY LANDSCAPE TYPE: Sierra Nevada mountains, giant sequoia forests, and alpine wilderness.
MAJOR NATURAL LANDMARKS: Mount Whitney, Moro Rock, Tunnel Log, and Crystal Cave.
SIGNATURE WILDLIFE: Black bears, mule deer, mountain lions, marmots, and Steller's jays.
VEGETATION ZONES: Foothill chaparral, mixed conifer forest, giant sequoia groves, subalpine meadows, and alpine tundra.
CLIMATE: Mediterranean with hot, dry summers and snowy winters; temperature varies by elevation.
UNIQUE GEOLOGY / ECOSYSTEM: Dominated by granitic rock uplifted by Sierra Nevada faulting, glacially carved valleys, and habitat for the world's largest trees.
INDIGENOUS HERITAGE: Originally inhabited by Western Mono, Yokuts, and Tubatulabal peoples who hunted, traded, and practiced seasonal burning. Their presence is marked by bedrock mortars and pictographs preserved in remote canyons.
HISTORIC SIGNIFICANCE: Established in 1890 as the second U.S. national park to protect the giant sequoia from logging.
FAMOUS LANDMARKS / TRAILS: Giant Forest, Congress Trail, Crescent Meadow, and High Sierra Trail.
WHAT IT'S KNOWN FOR: Home to the planet's largest trees by volume as well as towering Sierra summits.
ACTIVITIES: Hiking, camping, backpacking, caving, photography, and wildlife viewing.
AVERAGE VISIT DURATION: 1–3 days.
VISITOR TIPS: Carry tire chains in winter, bring layers, and explore early to avoid crowds.
HIGHLIGHT: The world's largest tree by volume, "General Sherman," located in the Giant Forest, stands 275 ft. tall and over 36 ft. wide at its base, symbolizing the park's grandeur.

Moro Rock, Sequoia National Park, California. Copyright © Lochlainn Seabrook.

SHENANDOAH NATIONAL PARK

OFFICIAL NAME: Shenandoah National Park.
STATE: Virginia.
DESIGNATION: National Park; est. December 26, 1935.
COORDINATES: 38.53° N, 78.35° W.
TOTAL AREA: 199,223 acres.
ELEVATION RANGE: 550–4,049 ft.
ANNUAL VISITORS: About 1.5 million.
OPERATING SEASON: Open year-round; busiest May–October.
GOVERNING BODY: National Park Service.
MAIN ENTRANCES / GATEWAYS: Front Royal, Thornton Gap, Swift Run Gap, Rockfish Gap.
PRIMARY LANDSCAPE TYPE: Blue Ridge Mountains ridge-and-valley system with hardwood forest and waterfalls.
MAJOR NATURAL LANDMARKS: Skyline Drive, Hawksbill Mountain, Old Rag, Dark Hollow Falls, Big Meadows.
SIGNATURE WILDLIFE: White-tailed deer, black bear, red fox, wild turkey, bobcat.
VEGETATION ZONES: Oak–hickory forests, mixed conifer stands, mountain meadows, riparian corridors.
CLIMATE: Humid continental with warm summers, cold winters, and frequent fog at high elevations.
UNIQUE GEOLOGY / ECOSYSTEM: Ancient granitic and metamorphic rocks uplifted 1 billion years ago; headwaters of the Shenandoah River; exceptional biodiversity within an eastern deciduous forest biome.
INDIGENOUS HERITAGE: Originally inhabited by Siouan-speaking tribes including the Manahoac and Monacan; region used for hunting and migration.
HISTORIC SIGNIFICANCE: Once Appalachian farmland; thousands displaced for park creation in the 1930s; major Civilian Conservation Corps restoration site.
FAMOUS LANDMARKS / TRAILS: Appalachian Trail (105 mi. within park), Stony Man Trail, Whiteoak Canyon, Marys Rock.
WHAT IT'S KNOWN FOR: Panoramic vistas, Skyline Drive, waterfalls, fall foliage, accessible wilderness close to the East Coast.
ACTIVITIES: Hiking, wildlife viewing, camping, scenic drives, and photography.
AVERAGE VISIT DURATION: 1–2 days.
VISITOR TIPS: Bring layers; fog and storms are common; arrive early for parking.
HIGHLIGHT: Skyline Drive's 75 overlooks provide unmatched views of Virginia's Blue Ridge Mountains.

Old Rag Mountain, Shenandoah National Park, Virginia. Copyright © Lochlainn Seabrook.

THEODORE ROOSEVELT NATIONAL PARK

OFFICIAL NAME: Theodore Roosevelt National Park.
STATE: North Dakota.
DESIGNATION: National Park; memorialized 1947; est. 1978.
COORDINATES: 46.97° N, 103.45° W.
TOTAL AREA: 70,447 acres.
ELEVATION RANGE: 1,940–2,850 ft.
ANNUAL VISITORS: About 700,000.
OPERATING SEASON: Open year-round; peak visitation May–September.
GOVERNING BODY: National Park Service.
MAIN ENTRANCES / GATEWAYS: Medora (South Unit), Watford City (North Unit), and Elkhorn Ranch Site access road.
PRIMARY LANDSCAPE TYPE: Badlands and mixed-grass prairie intersected by the Little Missouri River.
MAJOR NATURAL LANDMARKS: Painted Canyon, Buck Hill, and the Little Missouri River Valley.
SIGNATURE WILDLIFE: American bison, wild horses, elk, mule deer, pronghorn, prairie dog, and golden eagle.
VEGETATION ZONES: Shortgrass and mixed-grass prairie, cottonwood floodplains, sagebrush flats, and juniper breaks.
CLIMATE: Continental, with hot summers, cold winters, low humidity, and strong winds.
UNIQUE GEOLOGY / ECOSYSTEM: Multicolored sedimentary rock layers carved by erosion, featuring lignite seams, bentonite clay, and fossil-bearing strata supporting prairie biodiversity.
INDIGENOUS HERITAGE: Traditionally inhabited and traversed by the Mandan, Hidatsa, and Arikara Nations.
HISTORIC SIGNIFICANCE: Preserves the landscape that inspired Roosevelt's conservation ethic during his ranching years in the Dakota Territory.
FAMOUS LANDMARKS / TRAILS: Caprock Coulee Trail, Painted Canyon Overlook, and Petrified Forest Loop.
WHAT IT'S KNOWN FOR: Rugged badlands scenery, free-roaming wildlife, and its link to early American conservation history.
ACTIVITIES: Scenic drives, hiking, wildlife viewing, horseback riding, camping, and photography.
AVERAGE VISIT DURATION: 1–2 days.
VISITOR TIPS: Explore both park units; carry water, expect variable weather, and watch for bison on roads. Allow extra time for wildlife encounters and scenic overlooks.
HIGHLIGHT: Sunrise light over Painted Canyon reveals the vivid colors and layered geology that define Roosevelt Country.

Little Missouri River, Theodore Roosevelt National Park, North Dakota. Copyright © Lochlainn Seabrook.

VOYAGEURS NATIONAL PARK

OFFICIAL NAME: Voyageurs National Park.
STATE: Minnesota.
DESIGNATION: National Park; est. 1975.
COORDINATES: 48.50° N, 92.88° W.
TOTAL AREA: 218,200 acres.
ELEVATION RANGE: 1,100–1,400 ft.
ANNUAL VISITORS: Approx. 240,000.
OPERATING SEASON: Year-round; peak June–September.
GOVERNING BODY: National Park Service.
MAIN ENTRANCES / GATEWAYS: International Falls, Ash River, Crane Lake, Kabetogama Lake.
PRIMARY LANDSCAPE TYPE: Northern lakes and boreal forest.
MAJOR NATURAL LANDMARKS: Kabetogama Peninsula, Rainy Lake, Namakan Lake, Ash River Narrows.
SIGNATURE WILDLIFE: Gray wolf, black bear, moose, beaver, bald eagle, common loon.
VEGETATION ZONES: Boreal conifer forest, mixed hardwood, wetlands and peatlands.
CLIMATE: Humid continental; warm summers, cold snowy winters, annual precipitation ≈ 26 in.
UNIQUE GEOLOGY / ECOSYSTEM: Exposed Precambrian granite of the Canadian Shield with glacial lakes forming a vast water maze.
INDIGENOUS HERITAGE: Traditional homeland of the Ojibwe; archaeological sites reflect thousands of years of seasonal fishing and trading.
HISTORIC SIGNIFICANCE: Named for French fur traders who navigated its waterways in birchbark canoes during the 17th–18th Centuries.
FAMOUS LANDMARKS / TRAILS: Kettle Falls Hotel, Cruiser Lake Trail, Anderson Bay Overlook, Ellsworth Rock Gardens.
WHAT IT'S KNOWN FOR: Interconnected lake system ideal for boating, remote wilderness character, night skies, and Northern Lights.
ACTIVITIES: Canoeing, kayaking, houseboating, fishing, wildlife watching, snowshoeing, ice fishing, cross-country skiing.
AVERAGE VISIT DURATION: 2–3 days.
VISITOR TIPS: Access requires watercraft; bring maps and reserve campsites in advance due to limited on-land infrastructure.
HIGHLIGHT: Navigating the scenic chain of glacial lakes amid pine-clad islands, mirrorlike waters, and silent wild shores under brilliant auroras.

Rainy Lake, Voyageurs National Park, Minnesota. Copyright © Lochlainn Seabrook.

WHITE SANDS NATIONAL PARK

OFFICIAL NAME: White Sands National Park.
STATE: New Mexico.
DESIGNATION: National park; est. 1933 as a national monument, re-designated as a national park 2019.
COORDINATES: 32.7765° N, 106.1719° W.
TOTAL AREA: 145,762 acres.
ELEVATION RANGE: 3,887–4,116 ft.
ANNUAL VISITORS: About 730,000 per year.
OPERATING SEASON: Open year-round; hours vary with season and range activity.
GOVERNING BODY: National Park Service.
MAIN ENTRANCES / GATEWAYS: U.S. Highway 70 near Alamogordo.
PRIMARY LANDSCAPE TYPE: Gypsum-sand dunefield in a closed basin.
MAJOR NATURAL LANDMARKS: Lake Lucero playa; Alkali Flat.
SIGNATURE WILDLIFE: Bleached earless lizard; Apache pocket mouse; white insects adapted to dunes.
VEGETATION ZONES: Sparse grasses and shrubs on dune margins; minimal growth on active dunes.
CLIMATE: Cold-semiarid desert with low rainfall and wide temperature swings.
UNIQUE GEOLOGY / ECOSYSTEM: Gypsum from ancient seas eroded into the Tularosa Basin and formed the largest gypsum sand field on Earth.
INDIGENOUS HERITAGE: Inhabited for millennia; within ancestral Apache territory.
HISTORIC SIGNIFICANCE: Protected as a monument in 1933; designated a national park in 2019; home to Ice Age fossil trackways and ancient human footprints.
FAMOUS LANDMARKS / TRAILS: Dunes Drive; Interdune Boardwalk; Backcountry Trail.
WHAT IT'S KNOWN FOR: Brilliant white gypsum dunes stretching for miles under clear desert skies.
ACTIVITIES: Scenic driving, hiking, sand sledding, photography, stargazing, ranger-led programs, and full moon events.
AVERAGE VISIT DURATION: 2–4 hours.
VISITOR TIPS: Carry water, sun protection, and sturdy footwear; check for missile-range closures and shifting weather.
HIGHLIGHT: Shimmering white dunes in the Chihuahuan Desert formed by rare mineral and wind processes.

Sunrise, White Sands National Park, New Mexico. Copyright © Lochlainn Seabrook.

WIND CAVE NATIONAL PARK

OFFICIAL NAME: Wind Cave National Park.
STATE: South Dakota.
DESIGNATION: National Park; est. 1903.
COORDINATES: 43.55° N, 103.47° W.
TOTAL AREA: 33,924 acres.
ELEVATION RANGE: 3,435–5,013 ft.
ANNUAL VISITORS: Approximately 600,000 per year.
OPERATING SEASON: Open year-round; peak visitation spring through fall.
GOVERNING BODY: National Park Service.
MAIN ENTRANCES / GATEWAYS: U.S. Highway 385 north of Hot Springs; visitor center at natural entrance.
PRIMARY LANDSCAPE TYPE: Mixed-grass prairie and ponderosa pine forest overlying a limestone cave system.
MAJOR NATURAL LANDMARKS: Wind Cave, Rankin Ridge, Boland Ridge, and Red Valley prairie.
SIGNATURE WILDLIFE: Bison, elk, pronghorn, prairie dogs, black-footed ferrets, and coyotes.
VEGETATION ZONES: Mixed-grass prairie, pine woodland, and riparian valley corridors.
CLIMATE: Continental; cold winters, warm summers, steady winds; cave temperature averages 54 °F.
UNIQUE GEOLOGY / ECOSYSTEM: Over 150 miles of mapped passages and 95 percent of the world's known boxwork formations make it one of the most geologically significant caves on Earth.
INDIGENOUS HERITAGE: Sacred to the Lakota as the emergence place Washun Niya in tribal origin traditions.
HISTORIC SIGNIFICANCE: First U.S. national park designated to protect a cave and one of the oldest prairie preserves in America.
FAMOUS LANDMARKS / TRAILS: Natural Entrance, Fairgrounds and Garden of Eden Tours, Centennial Trail segment, and Rankin Ridge Trail.
WHAT IT'S KNOWN FOR: Complex maze-like cave system and intact prairie supporting free-roaming bison.
ACTIVITIES: Cave tours, hiking, wildlife watching, camping, and scenic drives.
AVERAGE VISIT DURATION: ½–full day.
VISITOR TIPS: Reserve cave tours early, bring a jacket, and keep safe distance (at least 100 ft.) from bison.
HIGHLIGHT: A rare meeting of subterranean wonders and living prairie life that embodies the timeless spirit of the American Great Plains.

American bison (*Bison bison*), Wind Cave National Park, South Dakota. Copyright © Lochlainn Seabrook.

YELLOWSTONE NATIONAL PARK

OFFICIAL NAME: Yellowstone National Park.
STATE: Wyoming, Montana, and Idaho.
DESIGNATION: National Park; est. 1872.
COORDINATES: 44.6°N, 110.5°W.
TOTAL AREA: 2,221,766 acres.
ELEVATION RANGE: 5,282–11,358 ft.
ANNUAL VISITORS: About 4.5 million.
OPERATING SEASON: Open year-round; peak visitation June–September.
GOVERNING BODY: National Park Service.
MAIN ENTRANCES / GATEWAYS: North (Gardiner, MT), West (West Yellowstone, MT), South (Jackson, WY), East (Cody, WY), and Northeast (Cooke City, MT).
PRIMARY LANDSCAPE TYPE: Volcanic plateau with rivers, forests, canyons, and geothermal basins.
MAJOR NATURAL LANDMARKS: Old Faithful, Grand Prismatic Spring, Yellowstone Lake, Grand Canyon of the Yellowstone, and Mammoth Hot Springs.
SIGNATURE WILDLIFE: Bison, elk, grizzly bear, gray wolf, moose, trumpeter swan, and bald eagle.
VEGETATION ZONES: Lodgepole pine forests, meadows, sagebrush steppe, and alpine tundra.
CLIMATE: Cold snowy winters, mild summers, and unpredictable mountain weather.
UNIQUE GEOLOGY / ECOSYSTEM: A massive volcanic caldera with more geothermal features than anywhere else on Earth, shaped by repeated eruptions and ongoing hydrothermal activity.
INDIGENOUS HERITAGE: Regarded as sacred land by Shoshone, Crow, Bannock, and Blackfeet tribes who hunted, fished, and held ceremonies here.
HISTORIC SIGNIFICANCE: America's first national park, established in 1872 to safeguard its geothermal marvels and wild ecosystems.
WHAT IT'S KNOWN FOR: Geysers, hot springs, wildlife, and volcanic landscapes.
ACTIVITIES: Hiking, camping, fishing, photography, and wildlife viewing.
AVERAGE VISIT DURATION: 2–4 days.
VISITOR TIPS: Arrive early, expect crowds near major geysers, and dress for rapid weather changes.
HIGHLIGHT: The rhythmic eruptions of Old Faithful symbolize the timeless, living power beneath Yellowstone's surface.

Grand Prismatic Spring, Yellowstone National Park, Wyoming. Copyright © Lochlainn Seabrook.

YOSEMITE NATIONAL PARK

OFFICIAL NAME: Yosemite National Park.
STATE: California.
DESIGNATION: National Park; est. 1890.
COORDINATES: 37.8651° N, 119.5383° W.
TOTAL AREA: 761,747 acres.
ELEVATION RANGE: 2,127–13,114 ft.
ANNUAL VISITORS: About 3.9 million.
OPERATING SEASON: Open year-round; Tioga Road closed in winter.
GOVERNING BODY: National Park Service.
MAIN ENTRANCES / GATEWAYS: Arch Rock, Big Oak Flat, South, and Tioga Pass entrances.
PRIMARY LANDSCAPE TYPE: Sierra Nevada alpine valleys, granite cliffs, waterfalls, and meadows.
MAJOR NATURAL LANDMARKS: Yosemite Valley, Half Dome, El Capitan, Glacier Point, Tuolumne Meadows, Mariposa Grove.
SIGNATURE WILDLIFE: Black bear, mule deer, mountain lion, bobcat, and Steller's jay.
VEGETATION ZONES: Foothill chaparral, mixed conifer forests, subalpine meadows, alpine tundra.
CLIMATE: Mediterranean with cool wet winters and warm dry summers.
UNIQUE GEOLOGY / ECOSYSTEM: Glacially carved granite domes, U-shaped valleys, and diverse montane habitats shaped by ice and erosion.
INDIGENOUS HERITAGE: Homeland of the Ahwahneechee, a Southern Sierra Miwok people whose traditions and place names endure.
HISTORIC SIGNIFICANCE: Among the first lands preserved for public enjoyment and a model for modern conservation worldwide.
FAMOUS LANDMARKS / TRAILS: Mist Trail, John Muir Trail, Yosemite Falls Trail, Glacier Point Road, and Mariposa Grove Trail.
WHAT IT'S KNOWN FOR: Towering granite cliffs, giant sequoias, and powerful waterfalls.
ACTIVITIES: Hiking, photography, climbing, camping, backpacking, and wildlife observation.
AVERAGE VISIT DURATION: 2–4 days.
VISITOR TIPS: Arrive early, reserve campsites months ahead, and expect high summer traffic.
HIGHLIGHT: Sunset alpenglow on Half Dome reflected in the Merced River.

Half Dome, Yosemite National Park, California. Copyright © Lochlainn Seabrook.

ZION NATIONAL PARK

OFFICIAL NAME: Zion National Park.
STATE: Utah.
DESIGNATION: National Park; est. November 19, 1919.
COORDINATES: 37.298° N, 113.026° W.
TOTAL AREA: 148,733 acres.
ELEVATION RANGE: 3,700–8,726 feet.
ANNUAL VISITORS: Approximately 4.9 million.
OPERATING SEASON: Open year-round.
GOVERNING BODY: National Park Service.
MAIN ENTRANCES / GATEWAYS: South entrance near Springdale; east entrance via Zion–Mount Carmel Highway; Kolob Canyons entrance off I-15.
PRIMARY LANDSCAPE TYPE: Deep sandstone canyons, high plateaus, and desert mesas.
MAJOR NATURAL LANDMARKS: Zion Canyon, The Narrows, Angels Landing, Checkerboard Mesa.
SIGNATURE WILDLIFE: Desert bighorn sheep, mule deer, peregrine falcon, California condor.
VEGETATION ZONES: Riparian woodland, desert scrub, pinyon-juniper forest, ponderosa pine at higher elevations.
CLIMATE: Arid to semi-arid with hot summers, cool winters, and brief monsoon storms.
UNIQUE GEOLOGY / ECOSYSTEM: At the junction of the Colorado Plateau, Great Basin, and Mojave Desert; known for Navajo Sandstone cliffs, hanging gardens, and Virgin River slot canyons.
INDIGENOUS HERITAGE: Long inhabited by Southern Paiute peoples who farmed and hunted along the Virgin River.
HISTORIC SIGNIFICANCE: Protected as Mukuntuweap National Monument in 1909; renamed Zion (pronounced Zy-un) in 1919 to preserve its canyon landscapes.
FAMOUS LANDMARKS / TRAILS: Angels Landing, The Narrows, Emerald Pools, Observation Point.
WHAT IT'S KNOWN FOR: Towering red cliffs, narrow slot canyons, and panoramic desert vistas.
ACTIVITIES: Hiking, canyoneering, rock climbing, and photography.
AVERAGE VISIT DURATION: 2–3 days.
VISITOR TIPS: Use park shuttles in peak season; avoid flash floods; start hikes early; carry ample water.
HIGHLIGHT: The Virgin River's deep canyon through Navajo Sandstone forms one of America's most iconic desert landscapes.

Angels Landing, Zion National Park, Utah. Copyright © Lochlainn Seabrook.

The End

HONORABLE MENTIONS
Our 13 Other U.S. National Parks

These thirteen national parks, though extraordinary in their own right, were set aside due to factors such as smaller size, lower visitation, limited diversity of scenery, or overlap with similar parks already represented.

1. Black Canyon of the Gunnison National Park — Colorado.
2. Gates of the Arctic National Park and Preserve — Alaska.
3. Gateway Arch National Park — Missouri.
4. Great Basin National Park — Nevada.
5. Katmai National Park and Preserve — Alaska.
6. Kings Canyon National Park — California.
7. Kobuk Valley National Park — Alaska.
8. Lake Clark National Park and Preserve — Alaska.
9. National Park of American Samoa — American Samoa.
10. New River Gorge National Park and Preserve — West Virginia.
11. Pinnacles National Park — California.
12. Virgin Islands National Park — U.S. Virgin Islands.
13. Wrangell–St. Elias National Park and Preserve — Alaska.

Valley of Ten Thousand Smokes, Katmai National Park and Preserve, Alaska. Copyright © Lochlainn Seabrook.

MEET THE AUTHOR

LOCHLAINN SEABROOK is a prolific lifelong researcher, historian, author, artist, and composer whose knowledge and experience span numerous fields. His remarkable productivity stems from his broad interests, decades of meticulous research, and an unwavering daily devotion to writing and creative exploration.

The idea of specializing in a single subject is a modern invention. In the spirit of the great polymaths—Aristotle, Isaac Newton, Benjamin Franklin, and Thomas Jefferson—Seabrook works across dozens of disciplines, with intellectual pursuits encompassing history, science, philosophy, religion, and the arts. The result is an expansive body of original writings that distill years of careful analysis into clear, accessible language for the general reader.

Rejecting the narrow confines of modern specialization, Seabrook views all knowledge as intrinsically interconnected. This integrative vision, combined with long hours of focused, solitary study and a rigorous work ethic, has enabled him to produce an extraordinary corpus of literature uniting the sciences and the humanities—a natural outgrowth of a lifetime devoted to inquiry, creativity, and the preservation of evidence-based history.

AMERICAN POLYMATH LOCHLAINN SEABROOK is a bestselling author, award-winning historian, and acclaimed multidisciplinary artist. A descendant of the families of Alexander Hamilton Stephens, John Singleton Mosby, Edmund Winchester Rucker, and William Giles Harding, the neo-Victorian scholar is a 7th generation Kentuckian, and one of the most prolific and widely read traditional writers in the world today. Known by literary critics as the "new Shelby Foote," the "American Robert Graves," the "Southern Joseph Campbell," and the "Rocky Mountain Richard Jefferies," and by his fans as the "the best author ever," he is a recipient of the United Daughters of the Confederacy's prestigious Jefferson Davis Historical Gold Medal, and is considered the foremost Southern interpreter of American Civil War history—or what he refers to as the War for the Constitution (1861-1865).

A lifelong litterateur, the Sons of Confederate Veterans member has authored and edited books ranging in topics from ancient and modern history, politics, science, comparative religion, diet and nutrition, spirituality, astronomy, entertainment, military, biography, mysticism, anthropology, cryptozoology, photography, and Bible studies, to natural history, technology, paleography, music, humor, gastronomy, etymology, paleontology, onomastics, mysteries, alternative health and fitness, wildlife, alternate history, comparative mythology, genealogy, Christian history, and the paranormal; books that his readers describe as "game changers," "transformative," and "life altering."

One of America's most popular living historians, nature writers, autodidacts, and Transcendentalists, he is a 17th generation Southerner of Appalachian heritage who descends from dozens of patriotic Revolutionary War soldiers and Confederate soldiers from Kentucky, Tennessee, North Carolina, and Virginia. Also a history, wildlife, and nature preservationist, the well-respected scrivener began life as a child prodigy, later maturing into an archetypal Renaissance Man and classical polymath.

Besides being cofounder and co-CEO of Sea Raven Press, an accomplished writer, author, historian, biographer, lexicographer, encyclopedist, neologist, publisher, editor, poet, polymathic creative, onomastician, etymologist, and Bible authority, the influential prosateur is also a Kentucky Colonel, eagle scout, entrepreneur, businessman, composer, screenwriter, nature, wildlife, and landscape photographer, videographer, and filmmaker, artist, artisan, painter, watercolorist, sculptor, ceramic artist, visual artist, sketch artist, pen and ink artist, graphic artist, graphic designer, book designer, book formatter, editorial designer, book cover designer, publishing designer, Web designer, poster artist, digital artist, cartoonist, content creator, inventor, aquarist, genealogist, ufologist, jewelry designer, jewelry maker, former history museum docent, teacher's assistant, and a former Red Cross certified lifeguard, ranch hand, zookeeper, and wrangler. A contemporary songwriter (of some 3,000 songs in a dozen genres), he is also a pianist, organist, drummer, bass player, rhythm guitarist, rhythm mandolinist, percussionist, electronic musician, synthesist, clavichordist, harpsichordist, classical composer, jingle composer, film composer (currently his musical work has been featured in 11 movies), lyricist, band leader, multi-instrument musician, lead vocalist, backup vocalist, session player, music producer, and recording studio mixing engineer, who has worked and performed with some of Nashville's top musicians and singers.

Currently Seabrook is the multi-genre author and editor of over 100 adult and children's books (totaling some 30,000 pages and 15,000,000 words) that have earned him accolades from around the globe. His works, which have sold on every continent except Antarctica, have introduced hundreds of thousands to vital facts that have been left out of our mainstream books. He has been endorsed internationally by leading experts, museum curators, award-winning historians, chart-topping authors, celebrities, filmmakers, noted scientists, well regarded educators, TV show hosts and producers, renowned military artists, venerable heritage organizations, and distinguished academicians of all races, creeds, and colors.

He currently holds two interesting world records: He is the author of the most books on American military officer Nathan Bedford Forrest, and he was the first to publicize and describe the 19th-Century platform reversal of America's two main political parties, namely that Civil War era Democrats (primarily in the South—the Confederacy) were Conservatives, while Civil War era Republicans (primarily in the North—the Union) were Liberals.

Of northern, western, and central European ancestry, he is the 6th great-grandson of the Earl of Oxford and a descendant of European royalty through his Kentucky father and West Virginia mother. A proud descendant of Appalachian coal miners, trainmen, mountain folk, and wilderness pioneers, his modern day cousins include: Johnny Cash, Elvis Presley, Lisa Marie Presley, Billy Ray and Miley Cyrus, Patty Loveless, Tim McGraw, Lee Ann Womack, Dolly Parton, Pat Boone, Naomi, Wynonna, and Ashley Judd, Ricky Skaggs, the Sunshine Sisters, Martha Carson, Chet Atkins, Patrick J. Buchanan, Cindy Crawford, Bertram Thomas Combs (Kentucky's 50th governor), Edith Bolling (second wife of President Woodrow Wilson), Andy Griffith, Riley Keough, George C. Scott, Robert Duvall, Reese Witherspoon, Lee Marvin, Rebecca Gayheart, and Tom Cruise.

A constitutionalist, avid outdoorsman, wilderness conservationist, and gun rights advocate, Seabrook is the author of the international blockbuster, *Everything You Were Taught About the Civil War is Wrong, Ask a Southerner!* He lives with his wife and family in the magnificent Rocky Mountains, heart of the American West, where you will find him writing, hiking, and filming.

For more information on Mr. Seabrook visit
LochlainnSeabrook.com

Praise for Author-Historian-Artist
Lochlainn Seabrook

"Bestselling author, award-winning historian, and esteemed nature writer Lochlainn Seabrook straddles multiple genres with ease, seamlessly weaving together history, science, politics, philosophy, and spirituality with the authority of a scholar and the flair of a storyteller." — SEA RAVEN PRESS

COMMENTS FROM OUR READERS AROUND THE WORLD

★ "Lochlainn Seabrook is a genius writer!" — STEVEN WARD
★ "Best author ever." — EMILY
★ "We get asked a lot what books we use and read. We don't do many modern historians, but we make an exception for some, and Lochlainn Seabrook is one of them. His works are completely well researched from original documents, and heavily footnoted and documented." — SOUTHERN HISTORICAL SOCIETY
★ "Looking forward to more Lochlainn Seabrook books, my favourite historian!" — ALBERTO IGLESIAS
★ "Lochlainn Seabrook is one of the finest authors on true history in this century. His books should be on every student's desk." — RONDA SAMMONS RENO
★ "All of Col. Seabrook's books are great. I have bought most of them and want to end up buying them all." — DAVID VAUGHN
★ "Lochlainn pulls together such arcane facts with relative ease, compiling these into ordinary prose that strike to the heart with substance, no fluff-speak. I am awestruck! Really. He is an inspiration to me. . . . He is truly a revolutionist. He dares to speak what others whisper; he writes with a boldness and an authoritative knowledge that is second to none." — JAY KRUIZENGA
★ "Mr. Lochlainn Seabrook is . . . the most well researched and heavily documented author I've ever read. His books are must haves. Everything he writes should be required reading! I assure you, you won't be disappointed. One simply cannot go wrong with his books. Mr. Seabrook is awesome! . . . I have never read any other author as well researched and footnoted as him. I've been in love with Mr. Seabrook for almost 5 years now. His quick wit and logic is enough reason to purchase his books. But the mere fact that he's so extensively researched is icing on the cake. Mr. Seabrook is my favorite, hands down." — LANI BURNETTE RINKEL
★ "My favorite book is the Bible. Lochlainn Seabrook wrote my second favorite book." — RICHARD FINGER
★ "I have a new favorite author and his name is Lochlainn Seabrook." — J. EWING
★ "Lochlainn Seabrook is an incredible writer and I love all of his books on the South. . . . His writing is brilliant. . . . I look forward to reading more of his masterpieces. Thank you." — JOEY
★ "It's hard to choose just one of Lochlainn's books!" — ROSANNE STEELE
★ "Mr. Seabrook, thank you ever so much for blessing us with your most enlightening works." — LAURENCE DRURY
★ "I recommend anything written by Lochlainn Seabrook." — HOTRODMOB
★ "Awesome books . . . by a great writer of truth, Lochlainn. Thank you so much. Keep up the great work you do." — WILDBUNCH19INF
★ "I love Lochlainn Seabrook's style and approach. It's not the 'norm.' What a miracle his books are. . . . He is a literal life changing author! Amazing books!" — KEITH PARISH

★ "I adore Mr. Seabrook's style and I love his books. I love an author that does proper research, and still finds a way to engage the reader. Mr. Seabrook does an admirable job of both." — DONALD CAUL

★ "Lochlainn Seabrook's books are much more well researched and authoritative than those eminently celebrated as being the authorities on the subjects he writes on. You can always trust to find the truth in his writings. . . . He does not rewrite history, but instead shows it as it is." — GARY STIER

★ "I love all of Colonel Seabrook's books. They are informative and enlightening, and his warm Southern hospitality writing style makes you feel right at home." — KEITH CRAVEN

★ "Lochlainn Seabrook's work is an absolute treasure of scholarship and historic scope." — MARK WAYNE CUNNINGHAM

★ "Mr. Seabrook's command of . . . history is breathtaking. . . . He deserves great renown—check out his books!" — MARGARET SIMMONS

★ "I love Seabrook's writings. LOVE!!! . . . So grateful to know the truth! Keep writing Lochlainn!!!" — REBECCA DALRYMPLE

★ "Lochlainn Seabrook . . . [has] probably [written] the best book on mental science in existence by a living author. Along with Thomas Troward, Emmet Fox, and Jack Addington, Mr. Seabrook is one of the top four mental science authors of all time, since biblical times." - IAN BARTON STEWART

★ "Glad I discovered Mr. Seabrook! . . . He writes eye opening books! Unbelievable the facts he unearths - and he backs it all up with truth, notes, footnotes, and bibliography! . . . He always amazes me! His books always see the whole picture. His timelines and bibliographies are incredible. He always provides carefully reasoned arguments! He's the best. To me I think he's better than the late great Shelby Foote! America needs more like Lochlainn Seabrook. I can't wait to own all of his books on the war someday. Everyone who wants the Truth, who seeks the Truth and wants the full story, should read his books." — JOHN BULL BADER

★ "I love all of Colonel Seabrook's books!" — DEBBIE SIDLE

★ "Amazing books for unreconstructed people who actually want to know the TRUTH. Seabrook's skill in writing and researching has no equal since the great Shelby Foote. If I could rate his books more than five stars I would." — CANDICE

★ "Lochlainn Seabrook is well educated and versed in what he writes and I'm impressed with the delivery." — THOMAS L. WHITE

★ "Lochlainn Seabrook is the author of great works of scholarship." — JOHN B.

★ "Thank you Lochlainn Seabrook for your wonderful books! You are the real deal! You are an amazing author and I love your books!!" — SOPHIA MEOW CELLIST

★ "I really enjoy Mr. Seabrook's books! His knowledge is beyond belief!" — SANDRA FISH

★ "Love Lochlainn Seabrook. Awesome!!" — ROBIN HENDERSON ARISTIDES

★ "Kudos to Lochlainn Seabrook who is a very good and informative professional truthful historian. We need more like him!" — AMY VACHON

Nurture Your Mind, Body, and Spirit!

READ THE BOOKS OF

SEA RAVEN PRESS

Visit our Webstore for a wide selection of wholesome, family-friendly, evidence-based, educational books for all ages. You'll be glad you did!

Artisan-Crafted Books & Merch From the Rocky Mountains

THANK YOU FOR SUPPORTING OUR SMALL AMERICAN FAMILY BUSINESS!

SeaRavenPress.com

Visit our sister sites:
LochlainnSeabrook.com
YouTube.com/user/SeaRavenPress
YouTube.com/@SeabrookFilms
Rumble.com/user/SeaRavenPress
Pond5.com/artist/LochlainnSeabrook

If you enjoyed this book you will be interested in some of Colonel Seabrook's popular related titles:

- The 50 Most Beautiful Aquarium Fish in the World: An Illustrated Guide to Nature's Most Stunning Freshwater and Marines Species
- The 50 Greatest Sharks of All Time: A Visual Guide to the Ocean's Apex Predators
- When Monsters Ruled: The 25 Scariest Animals of the Prehistoric World
- The Concise Book of Owls: A Guide to Nature's Most Mysterious Birds
- Rocky Mountain Equines: A Photographic Collection of Horses, Donkeys, and Mules of the American West
- Rocky Mountain Bison: A Photographic Collection of Bison of the American West
- The Cryptid Files Unsealed: An Illustrated Guide to the World's Most Terrifying Unknown Creatures
- The Concise Book of Tigers: A Guide to Nature's Most Remarkable Cats
- North America's Amazing Mammals: An Encyclopedia for the Whole Family

Available from Sea Raven Press and wherever fine books are sold

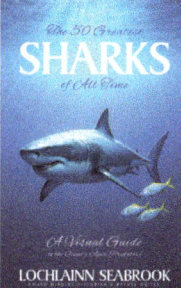

Please visit our Webstore for a complete list of Colonel Seabrook's books, as well as his fine art nature & wildlife photo prints, wall posters, and bumper stickers

SeaRavenPress.com

www.ingramcontent.com/pod-product-compliance
Lightning Source LLC
Chambersburg PA
CBHW042141160426

43201CB00021B/2360